It's Muddy And It Smells
Being Outdoors in Britain

Terry O'Connor

Published in 2020 by FeedARead.com Publishing

A CIP catalogue record for this title is available from the British Library.

Contents

This page is intentionally left blank as a tribute to Ordnance Survey grid square SE830220

Preface

This slim volume came about in the course of a few weeks in May 2020. That was, of course, the period of the Covid-19 lockdown, during which we all had to find ways of filling time that would otherwise have been spent visiting Barnard Castle. My friend Mike Sowden, writer and traveller *par excellence*, drew my attention to a challenge that he and others would be undertaking, to write a short book of, say, 25-35k words, in fifteen consecutive days. A couple of kilowords per day? Surely that's achievable, I foolishly thought. The choice of topic was something that had been rattling around in the cobwebby back-room of my mind for a while, to write something of an antidote to the overly lovely and picturesque accounts of the British countryside and to introduce some of the simple realities for those who may not be acquainted with ruralness. The lockdown period coincided with a spell of glorious Spring weather, of course, so lots of people were venturing out onto their local fields and footpaths. The time had come to put fingers to keyboard, daily, for fifteen days.

And this is the result. It is not a dreamy, philosophical account of being at one with Nature, nor is it a no-holds-barred invective against the horrors of intensive farming. It is opinionated, I admit, and some of the opinions may not be to your liking. But I like sheep more than horses and that's all there is to it. There are some bits of anecdote along the way, though I could pretend that they are essential experiential material, central to the topic. There are attempts at light humour and whimsy. There are some pictures, in black-and-white because of the mode of publication, though that has given me an excuse to play around with framing, contrast and so on. The individual essays can each be read as a stand-alone piece on a specific topic, though I hope that there is enough coherence between them for the collation to work as a book. That is very much in the mind of the beholder, so see what you think.

Acknowledgements

Many thanks to Mike Sowden for encouraging me to tackle the 15-day challenge, and to the many people who have accompanied me in the Outdoors over the years. Particular thanks go to Sonia, who has had over four decades of this nonsense up with which to put, and has done so most excellently.

On being Outdoors

Whether we are strolling, sauntering, ambling, striding, marching or yomping, walking in the countryside or just generally being Outdoors is one of those activities that most people will agree is a good thing to do as and when the opportunity arises. There are local and national clubs and societies devoted to it, not least the *soi-disant* Ramblers, who really ought to be a support group for incompetent public speakers. The supposed physical and mental health benefits are advocated by lifestyle magazines and by doctors who actually know of what they speak. A substantial retail industry is devoted to ensuring that we are adequately clothed and equipped. No doubt about it: being Outdoors is considered by many to be a Good Thing. Why? Our homes are mostly maintained at a comfortable temperature, are weatherproof, and are stocked with food and drink. Outdoors, at least in Britain, is mostly none of those things. And what are we actually doing, anyway, when we rent a day's parking, don our boots and cagoules and head off down a well-trodden path, usually along with numerous other people?

The percipient reader will have noted the use of an upper-case O for the word Outdoors. This is deliberate. It would be more conventional to refer to 'the countryside' or something similar when trying to summon up the places away from our residential clusters where we go for … whatever it is we go for. However, that term has to encompass landscapes as different as the reassuringly gentle rolling greenscapes of Middle England, the huge open skies of a Norfolk coastline, the wild mountains of Skye, a splodgy Devon farmyard or the bleak moorlands of Yorkshire. For such a range of different landscapes, any single term will be insufficient and too all-embracing. It will also be what a dedicated taxonomist would recognise as paraphyletic, for an explanation of which you're in the wrong place. Nit-picking notwithstanding, I have adopted the term Outdoors as a Proper Noun for the purpose of these essays, naming any place where asphalt and paving are in the minority, where plants large and small grow without necessarily having been deliberately planted, where there are animals other than dogs and cats. In short, where it is probably muddy and like as not it smells.

Definitely Outdoors. Dartmoor with gorse and clouds.

What is the attraction and what do we do there? The first and perhaps most obvious attraction is that Outdoors is Not Home. It is a change of scene, away from the familiar four walls and a sofa, away from the cleaning and DIY jobs that need to be done, away from the nagging telephone. For a while, we can put aside the obligations of everyday life, the To-Be-Dones that remain undone. If someone is unsuccessful in contacting us with some new hasslement, we can simply shrug and say that we were Out, away from the phone. For years, I laboured under the misconception that this was an important reason for people to head into the Outdoors, taking themselves out of contact. However, with the advent of the mobile phone, this theory has been soundly disproved. Walk any footpath virtually anywhere in Britain and there will be someone with their ear clamped to the phone discussing their business, divorce, criminal conspiracy or sex life at an audible volume. When I go Outdoors, having wisely left my phone at home, I am sternly reminded that it is a *mobile* phone and the general idea is that it should be with you. Why? So you can be contacted. What if I don't want to be? And so on. Exercise, that's the thing. People go Outdoors in order to exercise, where that verb encompasses everything from a short stroll with the dog to mountain-biking up Snowdon. When we go Outdoors, we mostly 'go for a walk', whatever that means to each of us in terms of age and fitness. The NHS regularly reminds us to look after our hearts, and regular exercise forms part of that regimen. And here we once again run into the challenge of finding the right noun for our exercise. Some things are obvious: if we heave aged legs over the cross bar and pedal off into the Outdoors, we are cycling. If we don the smart trainers and pad off up the lane at a gentle trot, we are running. Or jogging? At 65 years old, I jog now and then: 'running' is defined as going slightly faster than I can sustain for more than fifty metres. What about degrees of walking? I mentioned 'a short stroll'. What defines strolling, and is it faster or slower than ambling? Or just more directed? What about a saunter: how is that attractive-sounding activity to be distinguished? We have three apparent synonyms and that's without entering the darker worlds of rambling, bimbling or pottering about.

Ways of Walking:

Hiking	*Pacing*	*Wandering*
Marching	*Roving*	*Tramping*
Perambulating	*Progressing*	*Yomping*
Strolling	*Traipsing*	*Trekking*
Ambling	*Toddling*	*Stomping*
Sauntering	*Pottering*	
Roaming	*Bimbling*	

The English language does this sort of thing, of course, as a consequence of being a hybrid between Latin via Norman French and German via Anglo-Saxon. We'll ignore the contributions made by Urdu and Irish for the moment. What English generally manages to do is to give the different near-synonyms slightly different understood meanings, hence those comparative statements: I am a freedom-fighter, you are a partisan, she is a terrorist. Or, from my past day-job in archaeology: I excavate, you dig, he works for English Heritage. For some reason, we have failed to place generally-understood distinctions upon the many verbs for walking about. I walk, you stroll, he ambles? No, that doesn't work. The French, meanwhile, have the lovely term 'flâneur' for one who occupies their time sauntering around observing society. Almost by definition, a flâneur is urban: to observe society you must be among it. We need a rural equivalent, a term for someone who potters around in the Outdoors for no better reason that to observe it.

All this walking about in the Outdoors whatever we call it, underlines the exercise value. But does being Outdoors need to be active? Might we instead stroll, amble or saunter slowly, stopping frequently to look at something or to listen, occasionally back-tracking, sometimes just staring at the sky? If we are Outdoors for a couple of hours but cover no more than a kilometre or two, have we been for a walk? This is another area where tech has been more of a hindrance than anything, namely the marketing of devices that count your steps and download a line on some digital map. This is where you walked, they say, and this is how far and in how many minutes. Now, I quite accept that such a gubbins may be useful in circumstances where one is aiming for a particular fitness target or to walk a given number of miles in a week for charity. Or when my son uses his to say "I just did the Yorkshire Three Peaks in 8 hours 45 minutes. What's your best-ever time for it, Dad?" Fifteen minutes faster than you, since you ask. Where I get grumbly and exasperated is when these gadgets intrude themselves onto the wrists of people who are just out for a walk, simply enjoying the Outdoors in their own way. I have yet to see one that uses a symbol to show, for example, "And this is where you stopped to listen to that song thrush, and this is where you saw those gorgeous blue flowers that you mean to look up but won't remember to". It's all about distance, time and speed.

For some people, Outdoors is about challenging themselves, about having an adventure. Concepts such as strolling and stopping to listen to a bird are definitely off the agenda. Been there, done that; I fully understand what drives people, mostly young people, to undertake Outdoor challenges such as Duke of Edinburgh Awards. It may be hard work, physically uncomfortable and potentially dangerous, but that's the point. The contrast with the everyday is as marked as possible and the afterglow is difficult to achieve in any other way. None the less, I have the greatest respect for the fell-runner whom we encountered on top of Wetherlam, in the Lake District, many years ago. A big fell-race was on, and a steady stream of fit and perspiring folk was crossing the summit. One bloke stopped, looked around, and remarked to us "It's worth dropping back a few places to enjoy the view". Sensible chap. Maybe dedicated fell-runners and mountain-bikers should develop the habit of occasionally ambling slowly around their favoured routes in order to experience what they are not seeing, hearing and smelling as they thunder along in pursuit of personal-best times and calves like a bagfull of onions.

Lycra on wheels: Tour de Yorkshire

There are less overtly active ways of being Outdoors, of course, most of which are an excuse to sit still somewhere with a nice view. Victorian painters worked that one out, parking themselves in beauty spots to produce yet another watercolour sketch of Borrowdale, the sea at St Ives, Tenby by moonlight and so on. Sketching and painting constitute a fine excuse for a prolonged picnic. We have a fine watercolour of Rosedale painted by the architect Patrick Nuttgens. Pat was somewhat immobilised by Multiple Sclerosis but loved the Outdoors. Periodically, his wife would park him with wheelchair, easel, paints and picnic somewhere scenic, while she went off to spend her day elsewhere confident that he would still be in place when she went to pick him up. I'm not sure that this procedure would feature in training courses for working with disabled people, but it worked for them. For those of us who cannot draw or paint to our own satisfaction, let alone anyone else's, wildlife watching serves a similar function. Birds are the usual target, though some coastal locations offer the possibility of porpoises and other small whales. Far be it from me to describe birdwatching (usually 'birding' these days) as an excuse for a picnic with binoculars, but why not? Rather too many of the chaps, and it is usually men, who populate hides on nature reserves are a bit too damn serious in their pursuit of avian dinosaurs. Draw their attention to the way cloud shadows are scudding across that hillside in the distance and their response is likely to be somewhere between blank incomprehension and "Shhhhh!" And I say that as a former warden and a recorder for the British Trust for Ornithology! Smaller wildlife is increasingly attracting people to the Outdoors. Rockpooling has long been a good excuse to potter around on a beach and its appeal never fades. Taking children rockpooling or turning over bits of rotting log in a woodland is a great way to introduce them to Outdoors and to develop the habit of looking, feeling, smelling and listening.

Much as I love exercise, birds, snails, flowers and rocks, I would not argue for any one of them as being the primary reason to spend time in the great Outdoors. Walking, strolling or jogging along a country path or just sitting on the edge of a field should be experiences for all of the senses. The air will be moving over and past you, possibly briskly, bringing a range of sounds and smells that give hints of things happening out of sight, possibly far off. The breeze itself: is it warm or cold, dry or damp? What sounds does it makes in the trees or grasses around you? If by the sea, is the wind driving waves onto the shore, or blowing against the tide producing a lumpy, short sea? Walk a short distance and feel the texture of the ground, the sound that it makes with each footfall. Footpaths on the chalk hills of southern England have a particular ambience. The soil is thin, so the path surface is often bare chalk that crunches softly underfoot. Rabbits and sheep have reduced most of the surrounding vegetation to short turf, which may be dotted with small, stripy snails and occasional patches of yellow birdsfoot trefoil or purple thyme. There may be a skylark overhead. Above all, walking the broad tops of the Downs, there is the feeling of being a very small person under a big sky upon a huge convex sweep of land, like a pimple on an elephant's backside.

Being Outdoors is what we choose to make of it, but we can choose to make more of it than perhaps we do. Getting away from the routine is essential for many of us. As a retired man living in a more-or-less rural area, I have no routine to speak of, and plenty of opportunity for escape. That is a privilege, and one that I do not readily forget. Half-an-hour in the car takes us deep into one National Park, two hours and we can be well into either of two others. With those options suspended during the Covid-19 months, Outdoors shrank to the farmland immediately around home, but the pleasure of being Outdoors remained. The smaller frame required a focus on details: the smell of wild garlic, the sound of the wind in ash trees as they gradually came into leaf, ambling across the golf course without feeling the need to duck and cover. There was pleasure, too, in seeing other people enjoying the same local walks, knowing that the disruption to work and schools, whatever problems it had brought, introduced more people to the Outdoors and to the pleasure of simply being there.

...the pleasure of simply being there. Bolton Abbey, Yorkshire

It is a truth universally acknowledged that a chap set on some new activity must be in want of many quids' worth of kit. Whole retail empires have arisen on that premise, enriching their owners and shareholders by employing minimum wage staff to impoverish gullible customers. Temples to this devotional merchandising occupy the streets of, especially but by no means exclusively, towns in popular Outdoor resort areas. Is it all necessary? Given the nature of consumer capitalism, it would not be unreasonable to assume that a market has been spuriously created, driven by opportunity rather than necessity and sustained by marketing that preys on the increasing detachment between people and the Outdoors. Don't go out there without your Walker's Emporium technical under- and outerwear, your Bona Tramp boots and Co-Ordinates R'Us hand-held GPS unit, or you will surely get lost and perish. Or at least look like a total amateur.

Clothing is a good place to start. If the Outdoors calls and we head off for exercise or adventure, what do we need? Keeping warm and dry is the obvious objective, and the two things are clearly connected. Wet clothes rapidly become a means of personal refrigeration: uncomfortable at best and potentially lethal. Time was that the best advice was a sensible vest, thick shirt and woolly sweater. There is something both tragic and charming about the fact that Himalayan pioneer George Leigh Mallory was kitted out in wool and tweed on his fatal last days on Everest, and that those layers survived on his corpse for many decades in remarkably good condition, rather better than him. Those early mountaineers lacked only the modern materials that we wear today in egregious and eye-smiting colours. They understood how to layer garments to best effect. Today, fit young things who would not be seen dead in such a thing as a vest will pay serious money for 'base layer tops', which are, in fact, vests. Contrary to the cynical tone of this essay so far, I am a great fan of modern base-layers. The thermal ones, even the cheapest, actually do keep you warm and the polyester ones really do wick away perspiration. Compared to the cold, clammy embrace of a sweaty cotton T-shirt, they are a real improvement. But is it necessary to pay wedges of cash for a top in silk or finest Merino wool? Probably not, unless conspicuous consumption is what floats your figurative boat.

Another major advance in kit for the Outdoors is the polyester fleece. Yes, I know, they pill in the washing machine and shed microplastic fragments that eventually end up in the sea and get ingested by tiny marine organisms before working their way up the food chain into turtles and whales. As it happens, I have sources of raw sheep's fleece, am a capable hand-spinner, and could therefore produce my own pure wool sweaters. Eventually. Being pragmatic and also deeply suspicious about the way that pollution issues are delegated down to individual ordinary people to change their behaviour rather than tackling the big industrial polluters, I will continue to wear polyester fleeces but might just be a bit thoughtful about not washing them too often or too forcefully. Fleeces are warm, robust and mostly durable. They can be stacked into layers if conditions require, they dry quickly if they get wet and they weigh precious little.

The fact that I am not at the moment wearing a fleece is quite unusual.

We have established sensible ways to keep the upper body as warm or cool as conditions dictate and, furthermore, without resorting to high-price products. What about the legs? This prompts me to ask one of those fundamental questions about humanity: what madness persuades people that denim jeans are sensible outdoor wear in Britain? If the weather is hot, jeans enhance the baking effect, being dark enough to absorb every incoming iota of solar energy and thick enough to ensure that no heat escapes from the perspiring thighs. If the weather is wet, denim soaks up an inordinate amount of moisture, which then evaporates only very slowly so that the cooling effect persists long enough to become utterly vile. And should the jeans need to be washed, set aside a couple of days for them to dry. Oh yes, and the thick seams will almost certainly chafe and abrade your skin in some highly personal and tender locations. Denim jeans as Outdoor wear? Just say no. Polyester or polycotton is far better, often cheaper than jeans, and widely available. A word here about the curious garment 'cargo trousers'. This unlikely term refers to casual trousers with additional outsize pockets. Presumably the idea is that these pockets can be filled with whatever clutter may seem necessary: phone, wallet, spare change, house keys, sunglasses. Go on, try it. Now pull your trousers back up and think again. There is only a certain amount of weight that can be supported by a trouser waistband, especially on a hipless male waist. And that weight is well below the load capacity of a typical pair of cargo trousers.

Whoever originally designed them needs to get out more, preferably on a wet day in trousers laden with a kilogram or so of Kendal Mint Cake.

Trousers or shorts? That has to be a personal choice. Being descended from a flightless wading bird, I find my legs are much less susceptible to the cold than seems to be typical of most primate-descendants. Furthermore, Outdoors is usually muddy by definition and my legs wash and dry more readily than even the most sensible trousers. Shorts are thus favoured in all but miserable weather or if there is a likelihood of unavoidable stinging nettles. However, à chacun son, or sa, gout.

The highest-priced items in most kit shops are the bewildering range of waterproofs, anoraks, cagoules, jackets and suchlike. These serve the purpose of keeping the wind out of the underlying interstices and of keeping one dry. They used to be a nightmare of waterproofed nylon, which rapidly lost its waterproofing in a flaky shower of unpleasantness, or waxed cotton, which weighs far too much and smells of something dead. I should admit to owning a full-length waxed cotton raincoat, which certainly keeps me dry. I am reluctant to wear it too often in public for fear of being mistaken for one of the local grouse-murdering community, who partner the garment with a flat cap, a black Labrador, and an expression intended to intimidate. Fortunately, the development of 'breathable' waterproof fabrics means that we can now be dry and comfortable without making some kind of social statement. What I don't get are the up-market rain jackets with a zip-in detachable quilted lining. The idea seems to be that the jacket can be worn in mild or cold conditions, zipping the lining in our out as required. Yes. Or one could put on or remove a fleece or sweater, having spent considerably less money. Maybe I'm just missing something here. Incidentally, I hate hoods. Put the hood up and the wind promptly blows it off again. Tighten up the hood so that it is less vulnerable to the wind and all you can hear is your hair rustling against the inside of it. If, like me, you have tinnitus as well, the effect is really unpleasant and in stereo. So you loosen the hood a bit and realise that the person at your side is talking to you. You turn to face them and find yourself looking at the inside of your hood, possibly with your glasses now askew. Sod it. I hate hoods.

Footwear. This is where the pound signs really begin to spin in the eyes of retailers. Unfortunately for the customer, it is also one of those rare purchasing situations where what you pay is what you get. Cheap walking boots are not only inexpensive; they are almost invariably cheap in every sense. Uppers will remain 'showerproof' for about an hour and then become remarkably absorbent, soles will be more flexible than supportive and will rapidly wear down to reveal that they are actually hollow, and whatever attaches the laces to the boot will break or detach itself around the tenth time that you firmly tighten the laces. Oh, and the sizing will be mad, bearing no relation to conventional UK, US or Euro sizes or to human anatomy. Apart from all that, if you still want to take the risk of buying cheap boots, good luck. One of my sons had the misfortune to work for a certain well-known Outdoor kit supplier and was so embarrassed by the rubbish quality of their footwear that he would

quietly discourage customers from buying them.
Afford decent boots and look after them.

Despite the availability of more boots and sensible
shoes than one could shake a shoehorn at, folk still
take to the Outdoors in a remarkable range of stuff.
Flip-Flops, which Australians bewilderingly know as
'thongs' thus leading to wonderful misunderstandings,
seem to feature high on the list of desirable footwear
for newbie walkers. But not for long. The first
encounter with steep ground, a gritty surface, nettles
or fresh cowpats generally serves as a good learning
experience. Various forms of gym shoes and deck
shoes are hardly any better, however relaxed and
summery they look. Some people's footwear choices
leave me wondering whether *Homo* really is all that
sapiens. I once had to refuse to accompany a friend
who insisted that they would join us on the Snowdon
Horseshoe route wearing wellies. I don't care if they

are comfortable and keep your feet dry, they do not support your ankles and will be cut to pieces on rock and scree. Even good trainers have their limitations on those same grounds. Like it or not, serious Outdoors requires serious footwear. That said, walking sandals have a certain amount to recommend them, especially for people who do not mind wet feet and who have no sense of style or who are going to spend the day rockpooling. Guilty on all charges.

Having established that cargo trousers or shorts are not the sensible answer to carrying necessities while Out and about, we ought to consider backpacks, rucksacks, bumbags and other accoutrements. The choice can be bewildering and the 'get what you pay for' principle does not necessarily apply. Think what you might usually need to carry (i.e. not the maximum in theoretical extreme circumstances) and find a bag of around that capacity that feels comfortable on your back. Can you tuck a camera somewhere in or on it whence the camera can be quickly grabbed by you and nobody else? How about a water bottle? No, I don't want an integral water pouch that is well-nigh impossible to clean and which delivers dodgy water to my mouth by way of a suspiciously medical-looking tube. Yes, I would like the rucksack to be reasonably rainproof but just in case I will wrap any spare clothes in a plastic bag, which is cheaper than Gore-Tex. Is there a pocket into which a map will fit so you don't have to unpack the whole damn rucksack to check your whereabouts? These are simple tests, yet most rucksacks on sale in the UK fail them. Keep it simple and comfortable: that's the way with rucksacks. Having a somewhat eccentrically-constructed back, I am also a big fan of bumbags, preferably with a broad waistband that tightens up reliably and onto which a camera pouch can be attached. Americans call them 'fanny packs', which has at least as much comedy potential as 'thongs'.

Sticks and walking poles have been another growth industry, prompted in part by the notion that marching along with two Nordic poles, like a sort of ambulatory cross-trainer, is good for mind and body, and in part by the age and consequent joint condition of British ramblers. Twin-pole marchers have the additional advantage that they make themselves appreciably wider and more able to contest the right of passage on narrow footpaths. The single stick is an admirable means of prodding at unidentified things on the ground and for pointing authoritatively into the distance. Personally, I find a stick useful for balance and for relieving some of the strain on the knees when descending steeply. As modern sticks will usually telescope to fit in or on the rucksack when not required and are made of lightweight alloys, carrying a stick 'just in case' is no problem.

Much as I sneer at the proliferation of 'outdoor kit' shops and on-line retailers, I have to admit that modern materials and design have made substantial improvements in what is available compared to a few decades ago. There's just so many of them, all chasing the same market and doing so by exploiting low-paid sweatshop workers abroad to make the kit and low-paid workers in the UK to sell it. That's the nasty sting in the tale: the fact that some people spend twelve or more hours a day working in horrid conditions so that we can be comfortable and weatherproof during our

Outdoor leisure time, leisure time being something that the makers almost certainly do not have. Ethical shopping can become little more than ineffectual virtue-signalling, but if you can afford to pay just a little more in order to avoid giving business to the most exploitative of the retailers concerned, maybe that will make your Outdoor experience that little bit more pleasurable. And that is, after all, the general idea.

Fearless clothing: what we all need for the Outdoors.
Ghost sign, Cockermouth, Cumbria

The beaten track: Public Right of Way across a field in which a sown crop is just emerging.

The first phrase of Welsh that I ever learned was "Llwybr cyhoeddus", two inviting words that point the way onto public footpaths throughout Wales, usually indicating a gate or stile in a stone wall, beyond which a trampled path wanders mazily through soggy sedges and sheep dung towards a steepening slope, enticing the walker to thoughts of striding into the hills on a clear but not municipal pathway. The reality may well be that the path loses its identity among great tussocks of bracken or dissolves into a braided bewilderment of faint paths that diverge with no indication as to which is the main thoroughfare. Picking a plausible line, the walker marches on, only to come to a substantial wall or barbed-wire stock fence with no means of crossing it. Footpaths can be a wonderful thing or a cause of intense bafflement and frustration. For clarity, I am referring here to footpaths as they appear on the ground, not as they are mapped as these are often two quite different things.

One of the loveliest things about footpaths is their sheer diversity and way that they reflect local habits and history. West Yorkshire is a good county for the footpath connoisseur. Around the small mill-towns of Airedale and Calderdale, settlements that built up during the 19th century creep up the valley sides like rising damp. The main source of employment, t'Mill, was usually in the valley bottom, having originally utilised water power even if that were quickly replaced by coal and coke. Workers living up t'hill needed to get down t'hill to be on time for 6 a.m. shift at t'Mill. Look, that's enough faux-Yorkshire patois: you get the idea.

A network of footpaths ran across fields, over streams, and through the expanding settlements, sometimes just a trodden line through a pasture, sometimes a narrow, slab-paved ginnel between houses.

An earlier thoroughfare surviving as a ginnel in Otley, West Yorkshire. Photo: Sonia O'Connor

Interdigitated with that pattern would be the paths leading to the chapels, plural because even the smallest of mill-villages would have more than one flavour of Nonconformism. The result today is an intricate network of rights of way, many of them still paved by slabs or setts of local sandstone, sometimes

with a short flight of steps where the gradient increases. The mills are sometimes closed, often repurposed, but the footpaths remain as a fossil of that earlier landscape and how it was used by people.
We don't always think of footpaths as historic monuments in the same way as, for example, Roman roads. Almost any modern road, bridle path or footpath that runs dead straight across the land for miles, taking absurdly direct lines up and down hills is assumed to be a Roman road unless otherwise proven. The legionary approach to surveying seems to have been that light travels in straight lines and so do we. There is a charming parallel to this pig-headedness in the wall and fence lines that delineate the large fields of the 18th to 19th century Parliamentary Enclosures. These seem to have been laid out on a map or estate plan, somewhere indoors and a safe distance from the land itself. What appeared to be a rational place to set a land boundary was, in reality, a mad switchback up steep hillsides and across squidgy patches. Footpaths of older, more vernacular origins show their identity by avoiding doing any such thing. As a result, pre-existing footpaths on Enclosed land often take apparently irrational lines, going diagonally across the corner of one field thus requiring two stiles to be constructed when a more sensible line would have used that gate just 100m away. Don't blame the footpath: it was probably there first. There is a fine example close to my home. A wide path running between two fields meets a farm drive at right-angles, and the sensible walker would proceed onto the farm drive and turn right. But no! About 80m short of the junction, the statutory right of way requires you to step over the

right-hand fence, to cross the corner of the former playing fields of a private school and exit at the end of the farm drive. The school playing fields are now the gardens of a rest home, but the corner cut-off remains, a fine relic of earlier land use before either the school or the farm were built.

Relic. A former level-crossing gate encountered on a bridleway in Wales

A rather different form of historical landscape is preserved by footpaths and bridleways that have been established along abandoned railways. The 'Beeching' cuts to the railway network in Britain in the 1960s might be better blamed on the then Minster of Transport, Ernest Marples, who was, to all intents and purposes, in the pocket of the road haulage industry. Beeching was just the executioner, not the hanging judge. By getting Beeching to concentrate on passenger use on local lines, Marples ensured that lines that were important for local goods traffic appeared to be seriously under-used and hence closed, leaving businesses little alternative but to switch to road haulage. Brown envelopes all round! Not all abandoned rail lines date from that purge, of course. As industrial foci shifted, lines became more and less necessary, and wider access to motor cars certainly reduced passenger traffic on many lines. For decades, many of these unwanted lines sat derelict, becoming pleasantly overgrown and often becoming important refugia for wildlife, as well as for adventurous children. Now some are being brought back into use as traffic-free routes for walking and cycling.

At their best, former railways provide an excellent opportunity to be Outdoors with little likelihood of getting lost and safe in the knowledge that there will be no steep gradients to labour up or down. Many have become strips of woodland, perhaps with an understorey of bluebells and wild garlic in shadier places or wild strawberry on well-drained embankments. Even the materials of the embankment may add some historical detail. The Marpled railway behind my house is constructed on a track bed of the most widely-available local hardcore material: waste from coal workings. As a consequence, locals are warned never to build a bonfire on the edge of the embankment as there is just enough coal in it to catch fire and smoulder away underground. The only downside of the increased use of former rail lines for Outdoor recreation is that it leads to them being 'tidied up'. A narrow muddy path that winds between arbitrarily-positioned trees and shrubs is replaced by a wider gravel track that is pleasant underfoot in all weathers and not dangerously overhung or undermined by vagrant willows and brambles. Something wild is lost, accentuated if the new path is made accessible to cyclists, most of whom are polite and considerate but some are not and insist on their right to whizz along in a blur of lycra and self-righteous bloody-mindedness. A path that is over-managed becomes an artificial place and some of that may rub off on those who use it.

What makes a good footpath? Perhaps that is too much a matter of personal taste for any useful generalisation. Good signage is important. Most wanderers in the Outdoors have no interest in deliberately or inadvertently trespassing, so clear marking of footpaths serves the needs of landowners and users alike. So why do footpath signs get pulled down, painted over, blasted with shotgun pellets and so on? It helps no-one. Signs need to be in the right places, too, just as the walker is taking stock of the way ahead and wondering whereabouts to aim on that slight rise that obscures the view. Few things are more irritating than to be ambling along in the belief that this is the right way as indicated by that finger-post a half-mile ago, only to be brought to a dead stop by a barbed wire fence. Footpaths in woodland can be particularly problematic, as one cannot see the distance for the trees, and forest management activities often create apparent paths and roadways that bear no relation to anything that appears on a map. A woodland area near a friend's house in Devon has rendered itself walker friendly by simply placing posts at major path junctions with the OS grid reference embossed on the post. Anyone unsure of their exact whereabouts, which is a euphemism for 'lost', can quickly re-establish their point on the map or GPS.

Good signage. It is important to know the way to the Valley of Desolation

One solution to the challenge of not losing the way is to pick a route where getting lost is, at least theoretically, impossible. Canal towpaths and river banks are wonderful in that respect, whether they are meandering through attractive countryside or cutting an unusual path through a former industrial town. Canals have the added appeal of some industrial archaeology and plenty of ducks. Coastal paths are similarly easy: keep the sea to your left all morning, stop somewhere nice for lunch, keep the sea to your right all afternoon. At the time of writing, there are plans to make the whole coastline of mainland Britain accessible for coastal walkers. It's a lovely thought and a consummation devoutly to be wished, though currently some way off. Where the coastline tends to abrupt cliffs, a coastal footpath may not be for the faint-hearted, especially as coastal areas have a tendency to be windy. However, if safety requirements can be satisfactorily met, there is something uniquely enjoyable about following the margin between land and sea, taking in the changing moods and contrasts of each. Depending on the location and season, there is also a fair chance of the occasional descent to a small bay where ice cream is being sold and a bracing paddle to refresh the feet.

One of the oddities of coastal paths is the way that they distort time and space. Really, they do. Being an experienced Outdoor type, you consult your map or AI navigation gizmo, estimate the distance and time for the walk, and then find it takes longer and seems much further than the same distance would have done across almost any inland landscape short of the Black Cuillin ridge. Depending on the particular location, one factor in this is likely to be that field boundaries and the occasional small access road will run down to the cliff-edges or beach, necessitating gates, stiles and other inconveniences. Parts of the Pembrokeshire Coast Path are particularly tedious in this respect, with a ladder stile about every 100m (or so it seems) and, just as you get into your stride, a sudden plunge down into some bramble-ridden gulch followed by a meandering plod up the other side. Mind you, the scenery's gorgeous if you're in no hurry. The other factor is the fractal nature of coastlines. How long is the coastline of Britain? Measure it at a fairly coarse resolution, and you can get a fair approximation. That's 12,429km according to the US Central Intelligence Agency. Or 31,368km if measured at the high water mark according to a standard surveyor's method. That's a huge difference, and you might wonder whether the high water mark measurement includes every little wiggle of every embayment. Of course it doesn't. You might also wonder whether the CIA only measured the coast from Lands End to John O'Groats and forgot to come back down the other side. So how far is it to walk along the coast from, say, Scarborough to Whitby? Nobody knows. All we can say for sure is that it is further than you expect and will take you longer than you hoped.

In the year 2000, the UK Parliament enacted the Countryside Rights of Way Act, widely known as the CRoW Act. This established a right of access to unenclosed and uncultivated land unless there was a clear reason to exclude such access. The general idea was to allow people to wander freely over moors and mountains without having to, supposedly, keep to specified rights of way. In part, this was an obvious case of the law catching up with reality. In particularly popular tourist areas it was hoped that it would lead to people dispersing more widely across the Outdoors, reducing the pressure and erosion on major footpaths. That was a forlorn hope, for the simple and, in retrospect, totally bleedin' obvious reason that the existing footpaths were established along the routes that people wanted to follow. A change in the law changed neither topography nor the aspirations of walkers, fell-runners and water-colourists.

Armoured path, Rombald's Moor, Yorkshire. Not universally popular with walkers, and avoided by mountain bikers, hence track to the left.

Instead, some of our National Parks have embarked on a programme of armouring paths, replacing deeply-trodden tracks up and down hillsides with slabs of rock firmly pegged in place. To some, this is an abomination, an interference with the scenery and landscape. The same people probably object to decimal currency. Armoured paths usually have less impact on the land than the old trampled routes and are less susceptible to erosion when it pours with rain. Which, let's face it, it does. When the path across the notoriously soggy top of Rombalds Moor was armoured some years back, it was done with flagstone salvaged from repurposed mill and factory buildings. Every now and then, a stone occurs that bears marks of iron fittings or the tenon for some piece of equipment, like a craftsman or engineer who has been put out to grass in his retirement. Then a few slabs further on will be one that has been cleaved along the original bedding plane of the rock and now presents the lithified ripples of an ancient beach to the Yorkshire sky. Armoured paths are, in my view, a Good Thing in themselves and they can add some nice details to the Outdoor experience.

We should not take footpaths for granted. For one thing, there is always the possibility that they will be 'extinguished' for the convenience of a landowner or developer, reducing public access to Outdoors and quite possibly removing a humble reminder of how people previously used that particular landscape. They perform an important public service, keeping pedestrians and road vehicles entirely separated, and serve to entice people away from the spurious familiarity of roads and pavements. Nurture and protect footpaths and just occasionally stop walking along them. Sit down on the verge or on a convenient boulder and take a proper look at the line the path takes, how it is surfaced, what grows along its edges. Footpaths have characters and it is only polite to take the trouble to get to know them.

Granite tramway, Devon, now a footpath. The granite 'rails' show nicely through thick beech leaf-litter

Not getting lost

Where are we? We're here, as always. That may sound like two characters from a Samuel Beckett play pondering the futility of travel, actual or figurative, but it's also a good starting point for mulling over matters of maps, navigation and the vexed question of getting lost in the Outdoors. The purpose of maps, compasses, GPS and so on is to ensure that we know where we are at any given time in relation to, perhaps, our starting point and our intended destination. You can see how readily this elides into a 'life is a journey' allegory, so let's not do that. When we are Outdoors, how important is it to know our exact whereabouts? Obviously it is very important if we are in a landscape that is potentially lethal. To suddenly come upon an unsuspected cliff or raging torrent can put a crimp in the day's enjoyment. However, for most of us, most of the time, those are not the circumstances and an unintended diversion is unlikely to cost us more than a little time. Unless, that is, prowess at navigation really matters to us, so much so that if we successfully walk from A to B and back again, to have followed anything but the intended route is a matter for embarrassment and self-criticism. I used to be like that. These days, it is the journey and the time spent Outdoors that matter, not the achievement of a specific objective. The excellent nature writer Amy-Jane Beer once wrote of her wish to be able to spend days Outdoors just wandering, without having to consider for one moment where she would be at the end of the day. It's a lovely thought.

Some people get lost more readily than others: that seems to be a safe observation. We might add that different people get lost in different ways. Now, I'm no fan of pop psychology, especially when it comes to generalising about differences between men and women. That said, there do seem to be two quite different ways in which people navigate and find their way around a familiar landscape, and personal experience suggests that one way is more common in men, the other in women. Look, I'm just saying, that's all. Don't go reading a whole lot of sexual politics into that. Some people find their way around by going from one remembered landmark to the next. They're the ones who will tell you to follow the lane to the house with the green front door and a dog, then turn left through the gate and keep going to the small footbridge, you can just see the church from there so aim for that and… so on. The other sort will wave an arm in approximately the right direction and say "It's about four kilometres that way". In my experience, men, including me, tend to navigate by bearing and distance, women by landmarks. The landmarkers are more likely to be put off by a repainted door and missing dog, whereas the others are susceptible to getting turned about by meandering paths in woodland, emerging in bewilderment on the wrong side of a hill just as the tea-shop is closing.

How we build up and recall a mental map of an area is something highly individual and quite fascinating. Compared to many other species, we humans are remarkably inept at finding and remembering routes. Many species of birds and mammals migrate extraordinary distances, sometimes pinpointing an exact location after a journey of thousands of kilometres. Even snails have some capacity to find their way back home if they are taken a hundred metres away. We, meanwhile, get lost in an IKEA car-park. As with most human deficiencies, we use a technological fix for our incompetence. It never quite ceases to amaze me that if I can manage to prod the right bits of my smartphone's screen in roughly the right order, it will show me a map of where I am and a little blue dot that wanders along that map as I wander down the road. GPS technology is extraordinary, just short of magic to anyone who grew up before it existed. For the purposes of getting around an unfamiliar town, of finding that randomly-booked B&B that claims to have a view of the sea so why are we a mile inland, I will gladly hand myself over to the orbiting satellites and the little blue dot.

You guessed it: there's a but. GPS smartphone technology is not merely all but useless when one is seriously Outdoors, it can be genuinely dangerous. The accompanying maps are simple, intended to be followed by the majority of users. Besides, with the little blue dot pottering along, who needs detail? The Outdoors person, that's who. A smartphone app is unlikely to show footpaths, so the blue dot may appear to be isolated in a completely blank space, and certainly won't show contours, so the blank space between the blue dot and the car park may be an abrupt and gnarly hill or a sudden gorge. Will the smartphone map show you the recommended route around that obstacle? No. You're suddenly on your own. And to add to the fun, the unexpected hill is blocking your phone signal. And your battery's running

41

down. OK, I am over-stating the limitations of smartphone navigation a little, but it is only necessary to spend a little time Outdoors watching other people to realise that these devices are relied upon by many people and that reliance sometimes gets people into difficulties. Mountain Rescue personnel have volumes of anecdotes, often told through gritted teeth, of calls from people who have had an accident such as a sprained ankle and who cannot give their position to would-be rescuers because they have no idea where they are beyond the wandering blue dot. Don't be like them. Use a map.

Maps Ancient and Modern

Not being a person of faith or the avid follower of any particular political philosophy, I do not claim to have much in the way of firmly-held beliefs. One of the very few is that maps are a Good Thing. For anyone wishing to spend enjoyable time Outdoors, whether walking, jogging, painting or gawping at birds, a map is more or less essential, before, during and after. By presenting an area of land on a sheet of paper or plastic, a map encourages the exploration of options while still safely Indoors waiting for the rain to stop. Walks can be planned, good spots for picnics provisionally identified, the imagination can let rip. "Let's go to Wotsit-on-Sea. What's to see around there?" A map will tell you. So will Google, probably, but the map does not rely on advertising and will therefore give equal prominence to nice free places as to places that charge for parking, charge for admission and insist that you exit through some manner of gift shop. In fact, one of the advantages of modern Ordnance Survey maps is their conspicuous marking of tourist facilities, enabling the discerning Outdoor visitor to go somewhere else. They will also fill in the details in those suspiciously blank areas on the smartphone, warning us that in order to walk from the road to that promising-looking picnic spot will require crossing a patch of soft, wet ground across which no footpath is shown. Yes, there are blanks on Ordnance Survey maps. The kilometre square at grid reference SE830220, to be found on Landranger map 112, contains an electricity pylon and....umm, that's it. Officially the most boring grid square in Britain, SE830220 is near Ousefleet, which in turn is near Scunthorpe, which explains a lot.

Maps are good to plan and dream with, and valuable pieces of kit when in the Outdoors. Even if you are sure of where you are and where you are going (and which of us can truly say that?), what about that attractive path that branches off through the trees? No, that's not our intended route but look at how the light is dappling through the leaves: I wonder where it goes.

That's a moment to take out the map. Would it make a good diversion, or is that a walk to save for another day? One of the great strengths of maps is that they show not only where we are but what lies ahead and to either side. They facilitate exploration, enable rambling, and give us the confidence to wander off track for a while, knowing that we can find our way back. Thinking back, I can only recall two things that I learned at grammar school for which I have regularly been grateful. One is simultaneous equations: the other is map-reading.

The best of maps are also rather beautiful artefacts. The UK has the various Ordnance Survey map series, which have entered into the public consciousness as an element of the national heritage, even in the minds of people who never use maps. The history of the OS is long and fascinating, and the changing designs and scales of their maps constitute a topic in art history, quite apart from the technicalities of surveying methods. In fact, so ingrained are the OS standard symbols and colours that any other map design is inclined to look 'wrong'. This is obviously advantageous to the increasingly commercial OS, but means that other map-makers tend to be overlooked. I am a fan of Harvey's mountain maps in particular. Harvey's don't do national coverage, so a blank field near Ousefleet does not appear in their publications. They concentrate on areas of hills and mountains, and their mapping of the detail of rocks and crags is remarkably accurate and useful. They also map whether a footpath is clearly apparent on the ground or is just a theoretical line across a patch of terrain. That one difference from the confident OS footpath lines is really helpful. The OS tend to map the line of a statutory right of way rather than the actual footpath: the difference can be significant. Harvey's also print their maps on a waterproof material rather than encapsulating a paper map within two layers of plastic to produce something that is just thick enough and springy enough to be a pain in the neck to manipulate with cold hands on a draughty hillside.

OK, I love maps and will find almost any excuse to buy a new one. There is a rack stuffed full of maps in our porch and yet more of them, often dog-eared and tatty, have been retired to the loft, where they spend their twilight years yarning about days out and that time he got it wrong and went off in totally the wrong direction. They provide a means of planning and executing a day out, and a stimulus for the memory. A shelf-full of them also serves as a reminder that there is a lot of Outdoors out there.

An elegant sufficiency of maps. Almost.

Despite my advocacy of maps, I think that sometimes it may be good to get just a little lost, to kick against the habit of setting and attaining specific objectives. In the drizzly summer of 2019, I spent a few days in Snowdonia finding out that I am not as fit as I used to be. From the B&B where I was staying, I could use a small footbridge to cross a river then turn right and stroll through woodland to a small town where dinner and suchlike could be procured. One overcast day, just for the hell of it, I turned left at the end of the bridge, then right, then left...then just wandered off along a pleasant looking track into the trees. Around four hours later, I ambled into the small town from an unexpected direction, having passed a delightful day Outdoors in mature spruce woods, groves of young birch, green pastures, heathery moorland, listening to the birds, sitting on a rock. I saw only a handful of other people despite being in a National Park in summer. I had let myself get lost, without caring about my exact position and therefore, I suppose, not actually lost at all. Try it. There is something to be said for simply being Outdoors for the sake of it.

Weather is the day-to-day consequence of climate, the outcome of the Earth's rotation, tilt, precession, solar heating and energy exchanges between land, sea and atmosphere. It is entirely a matter of physics, and it really does not give a damn whether you decided to wear an extra fleece or not. None the less, anyone who spends time Outdoors in Britain will harbour suspicions that the weather is a malign, arbitrary and vindictive force, and will react with violent indignation on being confronted with the old adage that "There is no bad weather, only inadequate clothing". Of course there is bad weather. The only question is how bad and in what ways will that badness be manifested?

Let's start with wind. On a global scale, Britain is a distinctly windy place. This sceptred isle etc may not suffer the spectacular hurricanes or typhoons of the tropics and it is certainly not as windy as some parts of Antarctica, but for a mid-latitude place that would otherwise be described as 'temperate', Britain does wind rather well. We even have the admirable Beaufort Scale by which to quantify it, a quaint gallimaufry of waving branches and whipped-up waves that enables us to grasp the windiness of "Westerly 5 or 6, gusting gale 8". Francis Beaufort (1774-1857), incidentally, was Irish and therefore well-acquainted with fierce winds from infancy. His original scale described the force of the wind in terms of its effects on the sails of a ship. It was subsequently revised to describe sea, rather than sail, conditions and only in 1926 modified to use descriptions of land-based observations such as smoke rising vertically from chimneys, to small branches waving, to small dogs being blown about. I may have made that last one up. The 1926 revision was undertaken by Dr George Simpson who, at his death in 1965, was one of the last surviving members of Scott's *Terra Nova* expedition to Antarctica.

Force 6   22-27 knots 11-14 m/s Strong Breeze Large branches in motion; whistling heard in telegraph wires; umbrellas used with difficulty

Force 7   28-33 knots 14-17 m/s Near Gale Whole trees in motion; inconvenience felt when walking against the wind

Force 8   34-40 knots 17-21 m/s Gale Twigs break off trees; generally impedes progress

An extract from the modern Beaufort Scale. Note the insouciant "Generally impedes progress"

A strong wind turns a walk into a struggle, as it will invariably at some point in the day be blowing straight into your face. Hair blows around unless constrained by hats and hoods, which then blow off, and anorak toggles whip about and smack you in the eye. Deal with all of that, and you become aware that any excess fabric in your comfortably loose-fitting trousers is flogging about like the luff of an ill-disciplined sail. Force 6: trousers flutter noisily, sparrows fly sideways. So you tighten, restrain or belay any loose clothing or body parts, cancel any plans to take out the map, and stroll on smugly believing that you have this windy weather thing cracked. And maybe you have, just for a while, until the wearying, debilitating effect of simply being Outdoors on a windy day begins to make itself felt. Watch someone who has entered, say, a teashop or artisan cakemonger having been out in the wind. They stand almost shocked for a moment, then deliver a whole-body "Phew!" at the cessation of noise and the novelty of being able to stand upright.

That said, being Outdoors on a windy day can be wonderful. Whether bare-twigged or in full leaf, trees whoosh and roar, adding a percussion track of clattering as their branches judder together. Even open ground is noisy, different grasses hissing in their own pitch and tone as the air rushes through them. Waterfalls are blown sideways or even dispersed altogether so that they fall but fail to land, the water whisking away in a cloud of spray that may develop a local rainbow.

At the coast, the sea is pushed around and agitated, the outcome depending on whether the wind is on- or offshore, newly blowing or a three-day storm, a steady blow or lumpy gusts. Rough seas cause damage and cost lives, and should certainly not be treated lightly. Even so, there is something quite magnificent about a huge swell pushed up by strong winds peaking and breaking onto a rocky beach, all rolling green and mad foam. We should venture out more on windy days, not taking undue risks and suitably wrapped up against the blast, just to appreciate the sights and sounds produced by air masses balancing up areas of low and high pressure.

Wind becomes a different challenge when combined with some form of precipitation. Most of what falls on Britain does so as rain, but to the Outdoor connoisseur merely calling it 'rain' is a sad cop-out. How heavy is it, how penetrating, how large or fine are the droplets, is it falling vertically or slanted across by the wind? All of that and more besides differentiates rain from showers, downpour, drizzle, cloudburst or a fine soft day. It may be pissing, pouring or siling down, coming down like stair rods or raining cats and dogs. Rain needs its own agreed scale of terms: "Force 3 drizzle stopped play in the Test Match...". In the final analysis, though, only one question matters. Can I keep this rain on the outside of me? Obviously that is a matter for sensible water-proofs and due obeisance to the deity Gore-Tex. However, there is a particular form of fine, cold drizzle that seems quite tolerable when first encountered but which has the capacity to penetrate any forms of waterproof clothing, infiltrating along the seams, soaking its way into socks and up trouser legs.

You remain blissfully unaware that your defences have been over-run until that moment when you realise the sudden frisson down your back was caused by a trickle of cold water. This is not mere rain. This is insidious drizzle, and it is a Yorkshire speciality.

As with wind, the consequences of rain make it worth venturing out. Streams fill up, sometimes dramatically quickly, turning modest dribbles into dashing, foaming torrents. If the rain has been prolonged and the geology is suitable, there may even be springs suddenly erupting out of fields and roadsides. With warm summer rain, there is a tricky decision to make between donning the waterproofs, with the certainty of being too warm and sweatily damp within a half-hour at most, or removing as much clothing as social convention will allow and simply getting wet. Quick-drying modern fabrics make the latter option more and more feasible and attractive, turning a summer cloudburst into a memorable tactile experience.

Drop the temperature towards freezing point and precipitation undergoes all manner of changes. Water may have frozen gently into ice crystals in a high-up cloud then gently drifted down as snowflakes that partly melt before reaching the ground or spattering into your face. This is sleet: a vile intermediate precipitation that lacks the austere beauty of proper snow but adds the element of needle-like coldness to rain. Of all the weather conditions that should be acceptable excuses for staying indoors, sleet is top of the list. Not far behind it comes hail. A cloud fills itself up with perfectly respectable raindrops, which then freeze and, having frozen, freeze some more moisture onto their outsides until the icy lump is the size of a pea. At that point, gravity takes over and small pellets of ice plummet from the sky to assault any exposed human flesh below. I said pea-sized: occasionally, hail will grow to lumps the size of a golf-ball or more, causing significant pain and injury when they fall. I don't like sleet or hail.

Snow is another matter altogether, at least when it first falls. Even the most mundane of countryside is transformed by a white coating, the fine details of texture and colour smoothed out, the dark outlines of trees enhanced by contrasting tones. The familiar becomes, briefly, changed into something different and visually engaging.

Snowfall making the everyday seem unfamiliar

Walk onto that fresh snow and listen. In British conditions, footfall usually scrunches or squelches into snow, the pressure being enough to melt the snow underfoot into a wet, icy bootprint. But if the conditions are cold enough and the snow fine enough, it may not melt under pressure. Instead, the flakes slide past one another under compaction, producing a distinctive squeaking, creaking sound, which tells you that this is a *really* cold day. Snow entices people out to sledge and to snowball, which is all to the good if it gets people into the Outdoors. Yes, the trampling and the sledge-runs and the scooped up piles of snowmen soon destroy the virginal beauty of a fresh snowfall, but all snowfall is temporary outside the high polar regions. Better that it is enjoyed while it lays than just left to melt.

One of my most enjoyable and memorable days Outdoors in Britain owed its quality entirely to fresh snow. We had gone to Snowdonia for a weekend and arrived just after a heavy fall of fine snow. The day was windless, the sky completely blue, the temperature well below freezing. Any higher routes were obviously out of the question so we ambled gently around the lower flanks of Snowdon, out on the Miners' Path and back along the PYG Track. There was hardly anyone else on the hill and the silence was extraordinary. Clear winter sunshine and perfect snow: unforgettable, even though all we did was a few kilometres on tourist paths. Sometimes the weather can be wonderful.

There is wonder, too, in the formation of frost and ice. Frost in towns can appear to be nothing more than a whitening of roof-tops and maybe a patch of it in the local park. Venture further afield, and freezing weather offers some real joys. A windy hill-top, for example, may provide just the right conditions for ice to form on winter-dead grass stems, sheathing them in clear ice.

And if the wind has blown steadily during that formation, the ice is shaped by the wind direction, producing flattened forms around the grass, ice feathers that clatter and rattle like earth-bound wind chimes. Or find a pond that has clean, newly-formed ice covering the water and skim a stone across the ice. Get it right, and the ice resonates and whistles like something out of a radiophonic workshop. Another advantage of a sustained cold snap is that muddy and boggy ground freezes hard. Patches of terrain that are a squelchy nuisance to cross at almost any other time of year become an easy stroll. Until, that is, you hit a less deeply-frozen patch and go through into the sludge beneath, as one of our boys memorably found out at just the right age to survive, remember and learn from the incident. His loving parents didn't laugh. Not much. Winter high pressure, with clear night skies and hard frosts, can produce some perfect days for exploring Outdoors, with the bonus that daylight hours are relatively short so you don't have to feel guilty about heading back into a warm refuge around mid-afternoon.

And then there's sunshine, which we don't always think of as weather in quite the same sense as wind and rain. A sunny day in winter, one of those cold, icy ones, can be a real tonic even if the sunshine fails to raise the temperature much. By March, there is warmth in the sun, and a clear, bright day announces that Spring is finally on its way. The sensation of warmth after a long winter is something quite special, I think, especially as it is likely to be combined with early Spring flowers and birdsong. I don't sunbathe for the purpose of developing a suntan: my ancestry inclines me to burn. As my father put it "If you see a brown Irishman, it's rust". However, the feel of warm sun on the skin is one of life's pleasures, one of the few that have not yet been packaged and sold back to us.

A lovely sunny day, Orkney

Central to the enjoyment of weather Outdoors is the small matter of forecasts. Shall we walk over to Greendale tomorrow? What's the weather forecast like? For this we have to thank another pioneering Victorian, Robert Fitzroy (1805-1865), naval officer, hydrographer, sometime Governor General of New Zealand, and inventor not only of weather prediction but of the very term 'weather forecast'. Fitzroy wanted to reduce the awful toll of crews lost at sea by improving the prediction of storms. Even a few hours' warning could give a sailing vessel some chance of making shelter rather than being caught off-shore as a hooley blew up. He understood that changes in atmospheric pressure were crucial in understanding how the weather might be changing and successfully campaigned to have barometers placed at fishing and cargo ports. Robert Fitzroy was a humane and decent man who deserved far better than the debt and depression that finally led him to suicide.

Today's forecasts are remarkably accurate, despite the traditional grumbling about them, and readily accessible. Anyone heading Outdoors should check the weather, and not only by reading the often trivialised summaries. Weather charts are fascinating things, mapping the movements of great swirls of the atmosphere and drawing down that huge scale of information to the local detail of "Clouding over in the afternoon, with rain likely by tea-time". For the devoted weather nerd, the UK Shipping Forecasts are the real thing, a systematic prediction issued for regions around the coast, using a precise, concise vocabulary that has a poetry all of its own. Tyne, Dogger, Fisher, German Bight, Humber, Thames: yes, I probably can name the whole lot of them in order, including one of the largest – Fitzroy – named after the tragic Vice-Admiral in 2002 and the only sea area named after a person.

Weather, you see, is about more than just getting cold, wet or sunburned. Understanding it, measuring it and predicting it takes us into history and the biographies of some interesting people, and into grand narratives of the atmosphere sweeping and spinning around, of water evaporating off the distant Atlantic to fall as heavy showers on Headingley cricket ground. Good or bad, weather is part of being Outdoors, and should be appreciated, even savoured, not just tolerated.

Livestock: an introduction

Most of Outdoor Britain is farmed in one way or another, making it difficult not to encounter farm livestock. Even the vast arable fields of eastern England are likely to have sheep on them at some time. For the town-dweller, an unexpected meeting with the beasts of the field can be both confusing and alarming. I am on a public footpath: why are those huge animals with lethal-looking horns standing in my way, just looking at me? Are they about to attack? Should I talk to them? And so on. In fact there is much pleasure and reassurance to be had in getting to know farm animals, most of which will not actively try to kill you most of the time. What follows here is, obviously, very much a personal view, though it contains an essential kernel of truth.

Pony, Connemara. Don't trust 'em

I will start with horses, in order to get them out of the way. I don't particularly like horses and strongly suspect that the feeling is mutual. A number of women of my acquaintance who appear in other respects to be reasonably sane go soppy over horses, attributing to them all sorts of human qualities of majesty, beauty and loyalty. This is quite difficult to understand from, as it were, the outside. One possibility is that horses carry some sort of discreet parasite that can be passed on to female humans, in whom it causes changes to parts of the brain so that infected individuals believe that they must love and nurture horses, thus keeping the primary host well-tended and fed to the advantage of the parasite. If that sounds unlikely, it is only what cats manage to do by sharing *Toxoplasma* with us. Anyway, horses. Proper riding-type horses tend not to be kept on land that has public access because they are worth a lot of money. This is probably just as well as it reduces the chances of encountering a horse that will bite or kick you just for the hell of it. Less valuable horses tend to be chunkier, and these may sometimes be encountered leaning over a fence adjacent to some well-used footpath. The primary purpose of this behaviour is to encourage passing humans to hand over bits of food, because a handful of grass eaten from the hand is always preferable to pulling up a mouthful of grass one's self. Its secondary purpose is to lure naïve humans within biting distance. Horses may not have great pointy fangs like a tiger, but those comedy front teeth can be clamped around your shoulder very firmly indeed. And remember that if a horse owner should happen to see you being kicked, bitten, stamped upon or chased around the parish by their horse, it will be *your own fault*.

Special mention should be made of the feral horses of the Shetland Islands, the far-famed Shetland pony. These have all of the evil qualities of horses in general and no redeeming features whatsoever. Living out on the wind-swept moors of Shetland, they have evolved the remarkable ability to detect a sandwich or other packed lunch from a distance of several kilometres and have developed sophisticated techniques of distraction and intimidation to ensure that any such sandwich or pork pie is theirs for the taking, which it will be. A phrase used most regularly by visitors to Shetland runs something like "Ah, what lovely little ponies, aren't they just...GET OUT OF MY RUCKSACK YOU FOUL-SMELLING THUG!" True story: I was once working in an excavation trench in a large paddock that also contained two Shetland ponies. On hearing an unfamiliar grating sound, I looked up to find one of the little blighters was eating – yes, eating – the wooden handle of a spade. Not unreasonably, I shouted at the pony, which promptly ran off, still carrying the spade and, I swear, sniggering. As I may have said already, I don't much like horses.

Cattle, now are a different matter altogether. They come in a pleasing range of colours and sizes and a baffling range of behaviours. They are also the most lethal large mammal in Britain, having been responsible for some 74 deaths in the fifteen years from 2000 to 2015. In case that feeds into some stereotypic image of the dangerous raging bull, the overwhelming majority of those deaths were caused by cows. Most of the cattle that we are likely to encounter in Britain are cows, either in a dairy herd or a beef breeding herd. And of those cows, most will be the familiar black-and-white pattern typical of Holstein Friesians, known for short as Friesians in Britain and Holsteins in the USA. These are dairy cattle *par excellence* having been bred for frequent and prolonged lactations and a high yield. They can also be a bit skittish, in my experience, especially young heifers. I tend to give Friesians a wide berth and never, ever get between a cow and its calf. Conversely, if you find yourself faced with medium-sized reddish brown cattle with white woolly faces, relax. These are Hereford cattle, famously easy going. That said, any cow with calf will be protective, but in general a herd of Herefords is about as docile and chilled out as any cattle you are likely to encounter.

Amiable Hereford taking its humans for a walk

Cattle that you will probably meet when out in the wilder bits of Britain are Belted Galloways. These are pretty well unmistakable: small black cattle with a broad white belt around their bodies. They are hardy and adapt well to low-quality grazing, which is presumably why various National Parks and the National Trust have taken to using Belties to keep their upland pastures lightly grazed. When this first began, a farm vet friend was aghast, asking whether anyone in the National Park in question knew about the reputation Belties have for territorial aggression and random violence. An old stockman's saying has it that you can always tell a man who works with Belties – he keeps looking over his shoulder. Treat them with care and respect and keep your distance. The other cattle breed often let loose on hill pastures is the familiar Highland, a shaggy brownish critter, often with prominent horns. Given their appearance and Scottish origins, there is a tendency to expect these chaps to be aggressive and short-tempered: "See you, get aff ma hill!" sort of thing. In fact, they are rather good-natured cattle on the whole and if one strolls over to you it probably just wants its head scratched.

So that's cattle. Of course there are many other breeds, with their own particular quirks, but if you want a rule of thumb to minimise the chances of a disagreeable encounter with cattle, keep well clear of any cows with calves (and well clear of the calf, obviously) and treat any form of black-and-white cattle as potentially stroppy. Brown cattle, whether the red-brown of Herefords, the shaggy brown of Highlands or the golden-brown of Limousin, are likely to be fine. Incidentally, don't make the mistake of thinking that you can easily run away from a disgruntled cow: they can put on a serious turn of speed and corner rather well if the going is soft.

Which brings us to the delightful subject of sheep. These woolly beasties tend to be treated as a bit of a joke by people who have never had the pleasure of working with them at close range. My friend Tom, who farms sheep high up in the Yorkshire Dales, sums them up fairly concisely: "If a sheep can find a way to die, it will" and "Sheep are either fine or dead". In fact, most of his are fine most of the time, with the ewes lambing out on the hill in highly variable Spring weather and seldom needing any help at all. Rangy, shaggy hill sheep may look comical but they are, in the main, tough as old boots and highly competent at the business of being sheep. In our part of Yorkshire, the hill ewes are mostly what are known locally as 'mules', usually bred by a cross between the local Swaledale breed and a Blue-Faced Leicester tup (or ram). This latter breed deserves to win awards for the most consistently absurd-looking sheep. With their long necks and narrow, arched Roman nose, they look like a pantomime llama. Or a bit like the former French

President Charles De Gaulle. However, put the ridiculous tup to a Swaledale ewe, feed up the consequent ewe lambs as breeding stock and cross them with a stocky, muscular Texel or Suffolk tup, and the result is reliably twin lambs with the fast muscle growth of their sire, expertly raised by their mothers.

Sheep are useful. They will manage to find some sustenance on the most bleak and nasty of hill pastures. On lush arable land, they serve a useful purpose by grazing off the stubble and weeds after harvest, meanwhile spreading manure across the field ready for the following year's arable. Their main commercial purpose these days is meat. The wool has to be clipped but its value barely covers the cost of clipping, if that. This is a pity. As a hand-spinner, I find the range of variation in sheep's wool quite fascinating, from the very fine, soft Merino fleece to the long-staple of Lincoln or Wensleydale wool. Sheep's milk is developing a small but lively market, with sheep's milk cheeses being popular with discerning galactophiles. From the perspective of an Outdoorsy person, sheep are a decorative part of the scene and highly unlikely to be a problem. They may gather in a huddle close to a gate or stile if it happens to be sheltered, but will budge out of the way if approached confidently. Don't try shouting "Mint sauce!" at them. It means nothing to the sheep and just makes you look a prat. A ewe with lambs will be protective but is highly unlikely to act aggressively. Any charge is usually preceded by a stern look followed by stamping of one or both of the front feet. That is a warning, and is best heeded. Being butted by a sheep may sound comical but it hurts.

Unlike Shetland ponies, Shetland sheep are generally well behaved, though the Orkney sheep that live ferally on the wee island of North Ronaldsay are a different matter. These tatty animals spend most of the year confined to small areas of coastal turf and umpteen miles of rocky beach, where they feed enthusiastically on seaweed. Once a year or so, the sparse human population of the island and any capable visitors who happen to be available round up the sheep for a 'punding', getting the flock into a number of stone-walled enclosures (punds) around the island's foreshore, one for each grazing territory, for counting and clipping. A punding is variously fascinating, hilarious and exhausting. A line of people extends down the beach from the stone wall that separates beach from fields to the sea's edge and walks briskly forward, shouting, banging things together, rattling stones in a tin. The general idea is that the sheep take fright and run away from the advancing people, only to be alarmed by another few people standing at the crucial spot with pallets and loose gates to turn the sheep into a waiting pund. Simple, isn't it? Various things happen to make it less so. A group of sheep will decide that they are being coaxed out of their happy place, so they simply turn about and run straight back through and past the line of people. In theory I suppose they could be caught as they pass, but catching even a small sheep at full pelt on an uneven stony beach is difficult and potentially painful. Other sheep, probably some of the more experienced ewes, think here we go again and simply sit down. That's fine, you just stroll over and pick her up. Then realise that it is 400m to the nearest pund and you have your arms full of greasy, malodourous sheep and cannot see where you are putting your feet and...whoops, ouch, bugger. On one memorable punding, I went down the shore to scoop up two sheep that had avoided the rush by wandering out onto a seaweed-covered spit of rock. They obligingly waited for me to slither my way out to them, then one sat down and the other jumped in the sea and swam away up the beach. That was when I realised that sheep are not stupid at all. They are, in fact, highly intelligent animals but damned if they're going to let us know that.

Goats are surprisingly unlike sheep, despite some similarity of appearance. The best way to explain the difference is to imagine that the software in a sheep has been replaced by the operating system for a perky, medium-sized dog. Adult goats are often highly affectionate and actually seem to enjoy human company, and the kids scamper and play around rather like puppies. I do not mean to suggest that a goat will actually run and fetch a thrown stick or ball. Goats are not that stupid. They have a reputation for eating almost anything. This is, I think, an indicator of the intelligence of goats. Grass and leaves are all very well, but who knows what dining pleasure may be had from an old shoe, an abandoned dog lead, a length of orange baler twine. Sample everything, and repeat the sampling at regular intervals in case humans have changed the recipe for string since you last tried it. Speaking of intelligent animals brings us to pigs. A generation ago it was very unusual to encounter pigs Outdoors in Britain. There were plenty of pigs on farms but they were raised indoors in intensive units, often in conditions ill-suited to such behaviourally-complex animals. Today, it is more common to see pigs in fields, though unlikely that a pig field would have public footpath access. Should you happen to meet a pig on a footpath, the best advice is to step politely to one side and let the pig carry on to wherever it is going. My experience with pigs is that they mostly just want to get on with their lives and will not be looking for trouble. If you really annoy a pig it might eat you, but whose fault would that be? Outdoor pigs in Britain are likely to be from one of the minority breeds such as the self-explanatory Gloucester Old Spots or orangey, bristly Tamworths. One breed that you are unlikely to see, sad to say, are Mangalica pigs, regrettable because these beasts are covered with a dense, curly coat of hair and they look magnificent. They are originally from Hungary, though the resemblance to the now long-gone Lincolnshire Curly-Coat pig is quite striking. I am not making this up: they really do look like a pig wearing a sheepskin overcoat inside out.

Mangalica pigs above; Mule ewes below.

There is a stage-set 'Tudor' farm just North of Stratford-upon-Avon that has a couple of Mangalica pigs. They are provided with a perfectly satisfactory sty, in one corner of which is a fine weather-proof shed with a pig-sized entrance in one of its corners. According to the swineherd who was responsible for the pigs when they first arrived, they inspected the sty and the shed, conferred briefly, then set about chewing another entrance hole in a different corner of the shed, which entrance they then used exclusively. Pig feng shui? Who knows. The ways of pigs are mysterious, but of all farm animals, pigs really know how to relax and laze around, and that is a quality to be admired.

Footpaths often lead through farmyards, which range from sterile places of concrete and warning notices to mucky reproductions of a bad Edwardian painting with roses over the door and dung underfoot. And chickens. A farmyard is merely an animal factory unless it has a number of bewildered hens pottering about, stabbing their beaks at random bits of the ground and making a range of strange but endearing noises. Hens are just the right size to cuddle, and many of them actually seem to appreciate being tucked under an arm and gently hugged. Watching a bunch of them going about their business in a scruffy farmyard is about as relaxing as the Outdoors can get, especially if the farm in question supplies tea and cake. But don't take hens for granted. They are descended from dinosaurs and they knew this for a fact long before stupid humans finally caught up with the fossil record. Hens, let alone cockerels, fighting is spectacular, noisy and vicious. If a misguided rodent happens to get into a hen coop, it is likely to end up dead, pick-axed to death by numerous co-ordinated beaks. An angry hen can be a nasty piece of work. Fortunately, they seldom get really angry.

The one other farm animal that might be encountered on the loose in the Outdoors is the donkey. Despite my dismissive sniping at horses, I am rather fond of donkeys. That probably comes from having grown up at the seaside and remembering the small, gentle donkeys that gave rides on the beach. The complex smell of donkey and old leather saddle is still lodged in my memory from six decades ago. These days, donkeys are most likely to be met at a donkey sanctuary, though the occasional one is kept as a companion for an otherwise solitary horse. Donkeys lack the neurotic unpredictability of horses. A random piece of brightly-coloured litter blowing through a paddock is likely to send a highly-strung horse off on an alarmed and alarming, snorting canter. The donkey is more likely to eat the piece of litter. Years ago, I spent some time working on a provincial university campus in Tanzania, where donkeys acted as lawn-mowers. To be precise, these were not the little shaggy donkeys of my childhood, but rather grand African asses, elegant grey beasts the size of a large pony with a confident bearing. It is a nice thought that each little donkey we encounter in a damp British paddock secretly believes itself to be one of those fine animals.

So much for livestock as part of the British Outdoors. There is much more to be said, of course, and my particular take on the subject will not satisfy everyone. But if you need an excuse to sit down and catch your breath while ambling up a hill, watching sheep or cattle serves very well. And their dung attracts insects which attracts birds, so that can be a useful distraction, too. All in all, Outdoors needs livestock, just preferably not a gang of hyped-up Friesian heifers in the middle of a footpath.

Ass, being useful. Sokoine University, Tanzania

Birds and me

Birds are fascinating animals, yet thankfully only a small proportion of the people who are fascinated by them find it necessary or appropriate to take to print to express their fascination. The best of those writers are quite wonderful: engaging and articulate. The worst are tediously banal and anthropomorphic. I am quite capable of enjoying something about a robin without the little brute having a jolly name and being attributed emotions and characteristics that would embarrass a soap-opera bit-player. There he is, singing his little heart out! No he's not. He's issuing dire warnings to any other robin that comes anywhere near what he regards as his garden. That's not singing: that's "Come and 'ave a go if you think you're 'ard enough". Birds have featured as an important part of the backdrop of my life, and they are a good reason for hanging around in cold, bleak places Outdoors. First, of course, you have to notice them.

The earliest memories that I have of noticing birds are, probably as for most people, the birds that came to our small backyard where I grew up in Kent. Handfuls of stale bread and cut-up bacon rinds would be put out 'for the birds', which generally meant sparrows, song thrushes, blackbirds and starlings. Robins and greenfinches would turn up from time to time, but I do not recall other finches and tits. That may be because the food was always put out on the ground, and not on a raised bird table. Or maybe other birds just avoided the Isle of Thanet, which would be quite understandable. Mickey, our predatory cat, was in his prime, yet his morning collection of small corpses was nearly all small mammals, very rarely a bird despite the obvious opportunities. Maybe that early observation accounts for my scepticism regarding some of the more over-wrought concerns that cats wipe out garden birds in huge numbers. There were wood pigeons, too, though they rarely landed in our backyard. Their call was probably the first that I learned to connect to a particular bird species. Then came confusion with the appearance of another sort of pigeon, smaller and fawn-coloured. They were collared doves at the beginning of their dramatic spread across Britain. Seen from my small and local perspective, they were just another bird that had joined the party. Being close to the sea, there were gulls flying over but they never troubled themselves to solve the challenge of making a safe landing between wall, fences and washing line. There must have been occasional visits from less common species, but only one has stayed in my memory, and that very clearly. It was the cold winter of early 1963 and I was off school with bronchitis. I could almost add "as usual", as chest infections were a routine part of my childhood. Yes, I was that wheezing weed who was not good at games. It was around mid-morning, and my father was taking care of a poorly and bored child. He cut up a quantity of bread, precisely sawn into neat cubes as one would expect from a carpenter, and threw it out onto the thick snow that covered our yard. A flurry of cold and hungry birds fell from the sky, mostly the usual busy sparrows and strutting starlings. Then a plump and unfamiliar small bird came down, white in parts with darker wings and brownish patches. "Dad, what's this new bird?" It was a snow bunting, not a great rarity but I had no idea such exotic things even existed and to have a snow bunting pecking crumbs off the snow outside our kitchen window was exciting and wonderful. I remember my first snow bunting with greater clarity than subsequent 'firsts', perhaps because the setting was so appropriate. That memory came back to me with a thump years later, when I was at the top of Ben Nevis in snow, feeding sandwich crumbs to the friendly snow buntings.

We lived on the coast, so a regular and enjoyable excuse for a walk was in order to feed the gulls. I cannot imagine that my mother thought that the big flocks of gulls were in need of additional food, and the habit of taking them bread was purely for the entertainment value. To a small child, it was exhilarating to be stood in the midst of a cloud of squabbling, aerobatic black-headed gulls, tossing bread into the air to see it caught adeptly. Herring gulls, larger and more aggressive, would sometimes join in, but the small black-headed gulls were very much in the majority. It was getting to know those gulls which first taught me that some birds change their plumage through the year, the sleek chocolate-brown head of the summer birds fading and breaking up to an ashy patch in the winter. Feeding gulls is actively discouraged in many seaside towns today, local populations of herring gulls having become just a bit too smart and forceful. Personally, I admire their adaptability and the success that they have made of colonising 'our' habitat as we have built over theirs. This is not always a popular view. The herring gulls of St Ives in Cornwall are particularly adept. When my son James was in his early teens, he was ambling across the beach at St Ives with a doughnut in his hand (adolescent boys need to be constantly fed). He saw a herring gull flying straight towards him, beady eyes fixed on the doughnut. James waited, then at the last moment switched the doughnut to his other hand, like a matador sweeping his cape. His delight at seeing the gull soar past, empty-beaked, was short-lived as the bird executed a superb handbrake turn behind him and flew past his other hand, grabbing the doughnut en route. To the insult of losing his snack was added the injury of his father laughing delightedly and congratulating the gull. OK, herring gulls are big and stroppy and have pick-axe beaks that they use with precision, but you have to admire their insouciance and élan, non?

A familiar sign at the coast, dire warnings about the depredations of flying dinosaurs.

Garden birds and gulls were my first experience of birds, mainly in the context of feeding them. As I grew and spread my metaphorical wings, a range of shorebirds became an important part of the scene. Long walks on the beach, especially in winter and at low tide, became a regular part of my childhood and adolescence. I grew to appreciate the easy co-ordination with which a flock of gulls standing on the windy strand would take to the air if I passed too close to them, and the persistent scurrying of sanderling and other small waders at the water's edge, snatching scraps from each incoming, expiring wave. Turnstones always seemed more confident, muscling in and poking around the strand-line seaweed like habitués at a jumble sale, while dark, furtive rock pipits and chirping pied wagtails cleaned up around them. In retrospect, it was the shorebirds that first drew me to watch birds rather than just being aware of them as part of the background, and to appreciate seeing birds behaving as themselves, rather than responding to people.

I would love to be able to report that my nascent interest in birds was detected and nurtured at school, but it wasn't, at least not by the school. However, a nefarious quartet of us took to leaving the premises during lunchtimes, particularly during the spring migration. Depending on the season and the weather, we would target a likely place to see incoming migrants, pile into Neil's small car and head off in search of the year's first black redstart or winter's first Slavonian grebes. Following one of these forays, we were late getting back for a Biology lesson and scuttled into the lab somewhat abashed, with me soaking wet to the knees following a drainage ditch mishap. Asked to explain ourselves, Mark showed great presence of mind: "We were delayed trying to get an accurate count of a flock of yellow wagtails at Richborough" which, oddly enough, was true. A jaunt neatly became legitimate natural history fieldwork and we got away with it. The state of my trousers was not even mentioned.

My University years were spent in London, which is not prime bird-watching territory. That is, it was not in those days, before the development of wetland nature reserves around the edges of the city. However, I lived quite close to Regent's Park, with its resident herons and diverse decorative waterfowl. In case that sounds a bit up-market, I was not a resident of the grand Nash terraces that flank the park, but of a seedy patch just East of Edgware Road, not quite Paddington or Lisson Grove, disowned by Marylebone. Feeding a clutter of assorted ducks and coots was not quite the same as the seaside gulls of my childhood, but it gave some respite from the concrete and traffic. And there were occasional highlights. Walking in to lectures through the Park one morning with a friend, we were wonderfully distracted by a pair of great-crested grebes doing the full courtship display, standing breast to breast on the water, exchanging bits of water-weed and generally ignoring passers-by and gawping students. I have seen this display a few times since, but never at such close range or in quite such auspicious company. Reader, I married her. Despite the parks, London never felt truly like home. Seeing familiar black-headed gulls along the Thames merely reminded me that they adapted to the city more successfully than I did. One of the pleasures of our subsequent move to Cardiff was the far greater diversity of birds to be seen in Bute Park and along the Taff.

Garganey, West London Wetland Centre

Through all of this, I was an unsystematic birder. I kept no lists, no records of what had been seen where and when. To this day, I have no idea how many species of bird I have seen in the wild and I would not want to join the flocks of twitchers who will descend on some unsuspecting location to catch a glimpse of a rarity, adding another tick to their life-list. My rejection of twitching was validated one summer while staying on North Ronaldsay, in Orkney. A solitary Spanish sparrow dropped in for some reason or other, and suddenly the small island was a-clutter with folk in waxed cotton, all searching for a glimpse of this rarity. One group had even chartered a plane from South Wales: how bonkers is that? And while the serious twitchers focussed on the next tick on their lists, the sky was full of gulls, terns, waders, skylarks…

The closest I have come to serious birding was in the early 1980s when we first moved to Yorkshire, when I joined the volunteer warden team for a wetland nature reserve south of York. The real purpose of the reserve was to manage an area of traditional species-rich grazing land, but part of that management was to allow flooding in the winter so that the 'ings' became a haven for wintering ducks and geese. Monthly through the winter, the numbers of wildfowl would be counted and logged. That sounds quite straightforward and laudable, and gives no indication of the difficulties involved in trying to count, say 1000 wigeon on a windswept field, with chilled fingers and watering eyes. The little blighters will not keep still, and we would resort to estimation by area of birds. Count 20 ducks fairly exactly, then count up to 100 in estimated groups of 20, then up to 1000 in estimated groups of 100. Then, as you are not quite up to a final estimated total, something spooks the birds and they all take off. Ooh, you think, might that have been a peregrine falcon? You scan the sky in which a dispersed kiloduck is still whirling around: any sign of the predator that scared them into flight? No.

Despite the wildfowl counts, or maybe because of them, I grew very fond of those wetlands. My wardening skills may not have been up to much, though I did note the first evidence of ruddy duck breeding on the reserve, which some might regard as a mixed blessing, and confirmed breeding by goshawks. I also logged a rare sighting of the then Archbishop of York, in breeding plumage and accompanied by young. I carefully recorded that sighting in the reserve logbook, only to be told that "We don't record

Primates". Above all, though, I came to appreciate the bird soundscape. Winter was a gentle background of piping wigeon and redshanks, usually heard over the sounds of a brisk wind through the dead grasses. The noise level would rise and diversify into the spring, when it always seemed to me that the explosive peep of coots became more conspicuous. Why are coots always cross about something? Then summer would get underway properly and the dense riverbank vegetation would become a harsh chorus of sedge warblers accompanied by trilling martins. Breeding over, all became quiet again until wildfowl numbers began to build for the winter.

I still mark the seasons by changes in bird calls and song. Winter seems to drag on, with little more to enliven the garden than the disjointed twittering of robins and the plaintive contact calls of bullfinches. Then we hear the first male curlews displaying, their fluting calls a reminder that the days really are getting longer. Years ago, we conducted a survey to find out what it was that people most valued about the village in which we live. A surprising number of people wrote in that they really love hearing the curlews in late winter. Somewhere about mid-March the first migrants arrive, always introduced by hearing the first chiffchaffs. The display call of male chiffchaffs could not be described as musical or even particularly interesting. By about June, it has become positively monotonous. But in the cold days of late March, their metronomic tsit-tsat-tsit-tsat is as welcome as the daffodils. A few weeks later and the willow warblers start to sing their descending motif, like liquid silver. The first swallows arrive around the same time, then the transition of spring into early summer is marked by swifts hurtling through the evening sky, screaming, it often seems, just for the hell of it.

Goldfinch, eating my pension

As the chaos of child-rearing eased, I returned to the habit of feeding birds, putting out sunflower seeds in feeders suspended from trees at the bottom of the garden, then more recently closer to the house. For someone as tight-fisted and neurotic about spending as I am, the annual cost of seed and fat balls is quite significant, and only justifiable in terms of the pleasure that it gives. Although supplementary feeding of garden birds does make a contribution to sustaining populations of some species, I doubt that my contribution has saved many birds from starvation. Neighbouring fields and hedges are well supplied with berries and most neighbouring houses put out food.

Our local birds are spoiled for choice, but I feed them none the less. Few things brighten up a winter's day quite as much as seeing a bundle of long-tailed tits clustered around a suet ball, or the amusing spectacle of young jackdaws trying to copy them. They fall off, inelegantly, and it is difficult not to interpret the raucous squawks as laughter at each other's incompetence. Feeding the garden birds has become such a part of the domestic routine that I have even broken a lifelong habit and now keep a list. Fifty species, since you ask, not including birds that have been seen flying over.

Birds acquire an association with a place or a time, sometimes the first place where we encountered that species. I remember my first great grey shrike, seen on a bright, cold winter's day from a hide in which I was the solitary watcher. It was perfectly lit, just a few yards from me, and in no hurry to fly away. Or my first scarlet rosefinch, perched on a drystone wall in Orkney at a location that I could probably find again nearly 40 years later. Or my first black terns ... and so on. The associations may not be the obvious ones. To many people, ospreys are redolent of Scotland or at least of the craggier parts of Britain. When I think of ospreys, I recall a shadow passing across my breakfast in a hotel on the edge of the Arabian Gulf and looking up to see two ospreys directly overhead, hanging in the onshore breeze. Though memorable, more so than the hotel breakfast, there was something wrong with that osprey moment. Ospreys should be seen swooping over a lake somewhere categorically Outdoors, a Scottish loch or Cumbrian lake. Perhaps that is one of the reasons that I have never really taken to making lists or pursuing sightings of rarities. It is the context that matters, not just the bird, because the two things should be inseparable. It follows, then, that even quite a common bird in the right context can make a significant memory, if we just allow it to.

It was late summer, and the bracken was going brown on the moor above our home. I was sitting on a slab of rock, enjoying the sound of the wind and the view. A red kite, regularly seen in this part of Yorkshire, was soaring along the moor edge, systematically checking out the undergrowth for prey while balancing expertly on the updraft. After several minutes of this, it veered off and away. There was a faint noise in the bracken about five metres to my right, and a merlin took to the air. It flew around me at head height, still within a few metres, then went off about its business. Two moorland birds, neither of them twitchable rarities, but a few minutes that have stayed alive in memory. That's the thing about birds. They help us to absorb the moment.

In his celebrated painting 'Wanderer above the sea of fog', Caspar David Friedrich depicts a lone figure starkly outlined against a monochrome landscape of swirling greys and the darker, blocky forms of mountains. It is an image redolent of Western art's use of mountains as shorthand for a dramatic, challenging and ultimately uncaring world. Art aside, there is something about mountain scenery that thrills and excites us. Distant summits, dark crags, precipices, tumbling streams: the British landscape of mountain and moorland may be a little short on great altitude or scale yet still provides enough drama to entice some of us to walk its slopes and ridges. Others fail to see the appeal of plodding slowly uphill, probably in the rain, to join a number of other people at an ill-defined highest point with a magnificent view of the inside of a cloud. Putting it like that, what on Earth is the attraction?

Most obviously, there is the physical challenge. An individual peak or the crossing of a particular stretch of moorland attracts some people because it represents hours of hard work and the subsequent feeling of having achieved something that most people would not attempt, let alone attain. This is, I suspect, the only possible explanation for the large numbers of otherwise apparently sane people who flog their way to the top of England's Scafell Pike every year. It is a big hill, the highest in England, yet the walk to the summit is, by any and every route, tedious and dull. It must be the combination of having proved that, yes, I can do this and furthermore it's the highest point in

England that attracts walkers to the Lake District's least interesting major summit. Some will also be 'knocking it off' as part of a list.

List-makers and list-completers are a particular group of humanity to which I do not belong. Some people develop an interest in, for example, 1950s matchbox labels and then simply have to acquire examples of every case in that category and, furthermore, to keep a detailed list of the whole category against which to tick off their acquisitions. Some birders have this same tendency, and will keep lists of every bird seen in a given calendar year, at a specific location, in their entire lifetime. Summit-baggers fall into that same group, I suspect, aided and abetted by the numerous guidebooks that set out all the peaks in a given area, with recommended routes to the tops. Scotland took an early lead in this somewhat anal process through the activities of Sir Hugh, 4th Baronet Munro (1856-1919), who set out to list every peak and minor top in Scotland of at least 3000 feet (914.4 metres) above sea level. Why? One is tempted to suggest that as minor Scottish gentry, Sir Hugh had too much time on his hands. Anyway, he published his original list in 1891, since when there has been a rumbling ferment of arguments about whether this or that slight rise in a ridge constitutes a summit in its own right, not to mention various generations of resurveying that slightly amend heights and push this or that eminence on or off the list. Good grief. As of 2019, there is official recognition of 282 Munros and 227 'Munro Tops', qualifying elevations that are deemed to be part of a higher peak. And as soon as there is a list, there will be people who attempt to visit every single one of those summits, however remote, boggy and midgey of approach they may be. The first known complete Munro bagging by one man was attained by Hamish Brown in 1974, and in 2010 a fit and clearly over-focussed chap did the lot in just 40 days. Many, many more people will not necessarily complete all 282 Munros, but they will have a list tucked away somewhere and will take whatever opportunity to tick off another one.

In England, Alfred Wainwright (1907-1991) performed a similar role for the Lake District, though perhaps more unintentionally. The series of charmingly illustrated guidebooks that he produced between 1955 and 1966 describe and illustrate routes to the tops of 214 hills in the Lake District. He may not have intended that to become a definitive list, but in the hands of completist walkers it was inevitable that some would set out to visit every Wainwright summit. This is rather a pity, for at least a couple of reasons. The existence of the guidebooks has tended to focus walkers onto Wainwright's routes, exacerbating footpath erosion in places, and also because the books are simply too good to be used solely as lists. The illustrations are delightful and W's rather crabby dry humour comes across in the meticulously handwritten text. Furthermore, he was a rambler, someone who took to the hills as an escape from his mundane employment and less than happy marriage, and who would take his time, stopping to enjoy the view, rather than prioritising the summit.

Wainwright largely left Wales alone and the mountains of Brecon and Snowdonia lacked a 4th Baronet to catalogue them.

In the Carneddau, Snowdonia

Instead, the Welsh peaks were mostly catalogued by the extraordinary walker, photographer, perfumier and occasional cross-dresser W.A. Poucher (1891-1988; named William but known as Walter. No, I don't know why). Poucher's books on the mountains of Wales show his talents as a landscape photographer and his knack for describing a route, knowing exactly when the newbie walker would require some reassuring landmark to look for or some gentle warning of nearby squelch or plummet. As a research chemist specialising in perfumes, Poucher presumably also appreciated the many subtle variants of the odour of sheep droppings that characterise so much of upland Wales.

Some take to the hills and mountains, then, in order to tick another summit off their personal list. What do the rest of us get out of it? We gain a different perspective, both literally and figuratively. One of my favourite views is from part-way up the cliff of Pavey Ark, in Langdale, from which the view extends along the broad trough of Great Langdale, with its wonderful moraines, across the hills East of Windermere and the low-lying fields beyond, to the usually rather hazy ridge of the Pennines. Whatever else is going on in life at the time seems tiny, distant and slightly unreal.

Presumably that same change of perspective could be attained by driving to a car park with a bit of a view, but there is something about walking or scrambling to a mountain viewpoint that focusses the mind. The physical effort must be a part of it, reinforced, I think, if the location requires a certain amount of care in getting to it or in perching securely on that rock without falling an uncomfortably long way. That element of risk keeps us focussed on the here and now. On gentler, hazard-free terrain, the mind can wander and the worries and hang-ups that lurk in the mental mud can swim to the surface.

In recent years, I have come to understand how important the sound and texture of mountain and moorland paths are to me. Stepping off a paved surface onto a crunchy stone path that leads steeply upwards brings an immediate change of mindset, even if the walk is to be only a kilometre or two to a nice viewpoint. Going further into the hills and scrambling over scree and boulders is another change of disposition, requiring care over the placing of feet and hands. That in turn draws attention to the colour and texture of the rock, the presence of small plants and lichens, perhaps the sound of water trickling through cavities somewhere deep beneath the feet. Different geologies sound different underfoot: there is a world of difference between the soft clatter of limestone scree, the slither of wet Welsh slate, and the sharp, almost metallic rattle of some Lake District tuffs.

Jack's Rake, Langdale. A personal favourite, memorable for the roughness of its rocks

Walking and climbing in mountainous terrain holds the attention and fills it with different sensory inputs to those of the everyday. Add to all of that the way that even a gentle breeze can suddenly whip and whistle around a crag, the fraying and rippling of clouds over a hilltop and the high-up kronking of a raven, and you have something engaging and memorable.

Is that what we want from mountain and moorland: the experience of being somewhere different and somewhere detached from the everyday? Maybe so for the individual, personal experience, but how does that translate into society's management of these wild places? If Friedrich's Traveller were standing on a summit almost anywhere in Britain, he would probably be quite grateful for the sea of mist to conceal the forestry plantations, the burned and degraded grouse moors, and the over-grazed hill pastures. Timber, grouse and sheep are the three products for which most of our upland landscapes are managed, and each is in its own way destructive of the experience that visitors seek. To be fair, the days of dark, geometric conifer plantations are passing, though enough of them remain. Blocks of mature Sitka spruce plantation do little for the landscape and, when the trees are eventually cropped, leave hillsides reminiscent of a Paul Nash battlefield. Britain's hills urgently need more trees, but not like that. The farming of grouse for the shooting industry has become a serious issue in parts of Scotland and northern England, where huge areas are given over to this one species at the expense of absolutely anything that might compete with it for food or prey on the grouse or their eggs. Despite long-standing and unambiguous laws protecting birds of prey, buzzards, eagles, kites and harriers continue to be shot and poisoned on grouse moors, and successful prosecutions are rare. Too much moorland is owned by people who take the attitude that laws are for other people, the ruled not the rulers, whose land managers and gamekeepers know full well that a crime committed out of sight is unlikely to be investigated let alone prosecuted, especially when the landowner is likely to be a personal acquaintance of the magistrate and the Chief Constable. To be fair to the police, there is little that they can do without sound evidence and the support of the courts, and some regional forces have officers dedicated to combatting wildlife crime. Birds aside, grouse moor management includes the periodic burning of heather in order to encourage tender young growth to feed the grouse. It is not unusual for that burning to get out of hand, nor is it unusual for it to be undertaken during the first dry spring weather, just as snakes and lizards are coming out of hibernation and other ground-nesting birds are beginning to find territories. The end result is disturbance of breeding birds at their nesting locations, which is illegal, death by burning for adders and common lizards, and a charred hillside that is highly susceptible to rapid erosion with the next heavy fall of rain. Grouse moors are a blot on the landscape of our uplands in every possible way. Rant over.

What about our National Parks and other hilly places in the hands of conservation bodies such as the National Trust? What do they deliver for the Outdoor visitor? The National Parks are caught in something of a bind, for they have responsibilities to the visitors and to their resident populations. In other countries, National Parks are often huge areas of land where more or less nobody lives. Britain's Parks include appreciable numbers of residents, many of whom make a living from goods and services supplied to visitors. Management conflicts arise when, for example, someone wants to start up a business serving visiting adrenalin-junkies but others object because of the potential impact for a particularly well-loved view or on a popular footpath. Some of the conservation bodies are a mixed blessing, too, as they mistake the word conservation to mean "keep things just as they are". When that means maintaining an unstable landscape in which biodiversity and soil cover are steadily degrading because of over-grazing, that is not conservation.

Mountains and moorlands in Britain are not unproblematic. None the less they are places where a very particular form of Outdoors can be experienced, one that requires serious physical effort and care for one's safety. An Outdoors where getting lost really can have serious consequences, but where the everyday can be left behind for a few hours. I was going to end this essay with a brief pen-portrait of a few favourite spots, but which few? Quiet places away from tourist honeypots are special. My son introduced me to one at Malham Cove, one of the busiest locations in the Yorkshire Dales and likely to be heaving with people on almost any day of the year. Climb the stepped path to the top of the Cove, pick your way carefully along the edge of the cliff past all the people taking dramatic photographs. There is a place where you can cautiously step over the edge onto a small terrace, just far enough below and away from the crowd to feel private. Sit there a while with your feet dangling over the edge of the cliff and enjoy the sensation. On bigger mountains, Tryfan, an abrupt lump of rock in the Ogwen Valley of Snowdonia, is a favourite. The Heather Terrace route contours along the East side of Tryfan beneath dramatic buttresses and deep gullies. Scramble even a short way off the Terrace into one of

those gullies and you enter another world of echoes
and dripping water, steep rock soaring up to a small
patch of sky or, more often, into cloud. For something
a little more gentle in the Lake District, take the steep
but easy walk from Grasmere up to the rocky knoll
known as Stone Arthur. It's steep but not far. Now sit
down and enjoy the view: Grasmere, village and lake
almost at your feet, the Langdale fells ahead with
Coniston behind them, valleys running down to
Morecambe Bay to your left. Turn around, and a broad
whaleback ridge runs invitingly away to the top of
Fairfield. Tempted? Go on then. Enjoy.

Bootselfie, Black Cuillin ridge, Skye

On the beach

I grew up on the sandy, crowded beaches of North
Kent. To the thousands who cluttered the place up for
a few sunny weeks every summer, it was somewhere
to come, to escape from the grime of, mostly, London.
For me, it was somewhere interesting to be Outdoors.
For my formative years, being out of the house
generally meant being somewhere between land and
sea in an arc from Pegwell Bay around North Foreland
to the Roman fort at Reculver. It was years until I
found that there are other sorts of coastline, each with
their own attractions and attributes, but by then the
habit of spending enjoyable time walking the coast or
pottering on the beach was well entrenched. This is
not unusual. For a great many people, being Outdoors
means being at the coast, even though their particular
reasons are probably many and varied.
Seen on a map, coastlines are clear and definitive, a
line that divides land from sea. In reality, they are a
shifting, negotiable boundary. Twice per day around
most of Britain, that boundary moves as tides come
and go. In some places the tide may only mean a rise
of a metre or two in sea level, a bit more water in the
harbour, weed and barnacled rocks exposed for a
while at the foot of cliffs. In others, a falling tide
extends the land by many hundreds of metres as great
expanses of intertidal sand and mud emerge from the
sea, only to be inundated again a few hours later. In
some places, the tide can be seen, watched as great
swirls and bulges of water arrive and retreat around
headlands and into bays. A rising or falling tide rarely
moves straight up or down a beach. Watch the tide

repeatedly. Every couple of weeks or so, the tide comes in and goes out further than in the weeks in between. Even the high-tideline that might be taken to define the boundary of the coast shifts around as the moon coaxes the world's waters this way and that. There is something rather grand about tides. They shape small, individual patches of shoreline yet reflect global-scale processes in the oceans.

Coastlines shift on a longer timescale, too. As changes of global climate have altered the amount of water bound up in polar ice, so the amount of water in the oceans has increased and decreased. At the height of the last Ice Age, around 20,000 years ago, global sea levels fell so far that Australia and New Guinea were one land mass, Alaska merged with northeast Siberia, and Britain and Ireland were one, with an Atlantic coast a long way west of where it is today. The melting of that ice and the rising of sea level filled the Channel, Cardigan Bay and the North Sea, so tree-stumps emerge at low tide at Porth and trawlers drag up the remains of mammoths and other animals from the bed of the North Sea. In parallel with this sea level rise, parts of northern Britain, relieved of the weight of an ice-sheet, rose slowly as the Earth's crust found a new equilibrium. Many coastal locations in north-west Scotland have the remains of older beaches perched several metres above the present-day strand. Elsewhere, such as parts of East Yorkshire, soft sediments left by the ice-sheets make a low-lying, vulnerable coastline that is being rapidly eroded away. That's enough palaeogeography. The point is that the sea has not always been where it is now, that coastlines are temporary things.

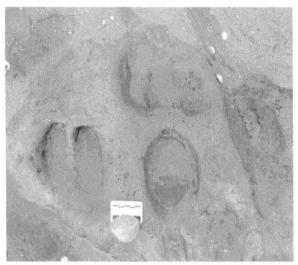

Prehistoric hoofprints exposed on a beach in Gower, South Wales

As you make your way down onto the beach, don't forget to look back at the land. The view may be nothing more prepossessing than a concrete promenade and a sad café, or it may be a line of cliffs stretching away. The coast offers almost our only opportunity to see the land in cross-section, to appreciate the immense thickness of the Chalk, for example, or the intricate layering of Jurassic sands and shales. North Sea coastal tapestries often include evidence of the Ice Age, in the form of thick layers of brownish clays mixed with lumps of rock from whatever land the ice had moved across. Robin Hood's Bay, Yorkshire, is a well-known place of resort for Outdoorsy types who like their seaside devoid of deckchairs and artificial amusements. It is a grand sweep of coastline, the Bay itself enclosed by rocky headlands and backed by Ice Age boulder clays from which pebbles and boulders erode out onto the beach. Hours can be spent by the rambling amateur geologist picking over these rocks, recognising dolerites from the Whin Sill, some 150km to the north, Shap Fell granites from the lost world of Westmoreland, even Scandinavian porphyry rocks. Other locations may yield fossils from the cliffs, but do be aware that cliffs fall down from time to time and it is as well not to be near them when that happens.

Huge intertidal zone with sculpted sand, Pembrokeshire

Between the highest and lowest of tides is what ecologists call the intertidal zone, a landscape entirely of itself, neither land nor sea, with its own distinctive geography and ecology. This is the place of sandbanks and swales, rock platforms, mussel beds, weed-draped gullies and rockpools, the exploration of which requires a little effort and care. Where the intertidal zone is mostly sand, it may be a very long walk from high to low water mark, apparently seeing very little along the way. Think again. Very few such beaches slope steadily from high to low: there will be rises and falls, reflecting the swirl of tidal currents, possibly leaving curving pools of water between tides. The sand surface will vary, billiard-table smooth in places, deeply sculpted into arcuate ripples in others. The sand texture will vary, sometimes coarse and gritty, sometimes as fine as flour, sometimes surprisingly firm and elsewhere softly yielding. The last dribble of retreating water may sort the fine and coarse particles as it goes, leaving stripes and deltas of coarser material, rich in broken shells and bits of crab carapace. A huge expanse of sandy beach may appear uniform and without interest, but is far from it. There will be wildlife, too, and not just the handful of gulls that hang around in small groups like teenagers waiting for something to happen. Most sandy beaches will have patches where the smooth surface is pimpled by lugworm casts, those wriggly squirls of defaecated sand that mark one end of the worm's burrow. Look around the cast, a hand's breadth away from it, and you may find a shallow, conical depression. That is the other end of the horseshoe-shaped burrow, between which the worm passes its time extracting oxygen and particles of food. Not every small depression marks a lugworm burrow. There may be razor shells, delicious molluscs that hide in the sand close to the low tide mark but often give away their position in response to clumpy footfalls by squirting water into the air. It's just what they do: it's not personal. Some beaches house a burrowing sea-urchin known colloquially as a sea-potato, from a supposed and entirely fanciful resemblance to the vegetable, the burrows of which have a distinctive entrance resembling the clubs motif on a playing card. Other critters may have left tracks on the sand surface: the broad, meandering furrow of a periwinkle or the complex pattern left by a scuttling crab. Sandy beaches may lack the immediate attraction of rockpools and boulders, but they repay slow, patient ambling, eyes open, head down, imagination turned up to eleven.

In comparison, rocky shores wear their attractions on the surface, positively flaunting their potential for a few lazy Outdoor hours. One word of practical advice. If you are venturing onto a rocky shore, wear something on your feet or be prepared for a world of pain. If the barnacles don't get you, the mussel shells will and the sensation of salt water finding its way into a sharply exfoliated foot is really not nice. Poke around under rocks, behind weed and in the backs of damp crevices, and there will be crabs, shrimps, possibly small fish, blobby sea anemones, maybe sea squirts, starfish and an assortment of shelled beasties. Some rocky shores are inhabited by a diverse fauna of molluscs, both bivalves and gastropods, while others may have only two or three species but those in huge numbers. The diversity is engaging. Crabs invite capture, risking a nip from the pincers that they wave aggressively. In fact, the common shore crabs are all show, giving it large on the pincer front whilst backing away from you into some hidey-hole. Not so the velvet swimmer crab: these red-eyed little psychopaths will actively go for you with malicious intent. If they ever get the hang of broken bottles, no shore will be safe. Meanwhile, the tide has turned and is coming back in, neatly encircling the rocky spit on which you are obliviously pottering and requiring a brisk wade back to the beach, trying to look as if that was your intention all along.

Shore crab. Note the practised skill with which this beast is handled. Photo: Sonia O'Connor

One further difference to note between sandy and rocky shores is the colour of the water. Waves and currents will pick up and shift quantities of fine sand and silt, giving the water an opaque khaki colour that always looks distinctly unhealthy, possibly because sewage pollution has much the same visible effect. Boatmen looking out for shallow water over sandbanks sometimes refer to 'yeasty' water, a usefully descriptive term. In contrast, waves coming in over rocks are often of a transparent greeny-blue, far more appealing to the eye. Looking over the sea from a distance, perhaps from adjacent cliffs, the surface varies in colour from genuinely blue through various shades of green and grey to lilacs, with the dark shadows of clouds providing a contrast. Any waves that may have been generated by the wind will add texture to the colours, perhaps with a highlight of foam at the crest. It is little wonder that so many artists have tried to capture the colours and moods of the sea, and no surprise that few have really succeeded.

This is all detail. The point of being Outdoors is in order to absorb the whole sensory experience. As you walk across a beach or intertidal shore, listen to the sounds made by your feet, rattling over shingle, scrunching through sand and dry seaweed, splashing through shallow water, slipping and popping over fresh wrack. Beaches often smell, too. The odour of cheap suntan lotion and candy floss takes me back to childhood summer days. Head off down the beach to get away from it, get in among the rocks near the low water mark and an altogether different smell hits the nostrils. This is the 'crumb-of-bread' sponge, *Halichondria panicea*. The common name presumably refers to its bread-like texture and not its greeny-yellow colour. Sadly, the smell has little to do with freshly-baked bread or inviting morning toast: it is indescribably chemical, like something dead, something that was barely alive in the first place. OK, that's not really inviting, is it?

A boulder beach, difficult to explore but rewarding

Some coastal locations stick in the memory. At the
north end of the main island of Shetland, at a place
called Fethaland, there is a pair of small bays separated
by a narrow isthmus of sand and stones. At the end of
the isthmus is a rocky headland with a lighthouse.
Beyond that is the Atlantic Ocean, all the way to the
Arctic. The knowledge of that location, that last point
on a body of land, itself far away from the majority of
Britain, gives those two little bays a certain quality. To
the west of the isthmus, the foreshore is a pile of huge
boulders that tumble steeply to the sea. When wet,
which they usually are by sea spray or rain, the
boulders have a silvery sheen, almost like pewter,
which they borrow from minerals in the metamorphic
rocks of this end of Shetland. This is the weather-
beaten side of the isthmus, where the westerly and
northerly winds drive the sea ashore on a long, long

reach that builds waves up to a size that can toss a ton of rock up the beach. On a calm day, it is also a good place to watch for seals and otters. The boulders provide many nooks and crannies for crabs and butterfish, which otters catch skilfully and devour voraciously.

The bay on the east side is sheltered from the westerly winds and gets some protection from northerlies from the headland. As a consequence, it is a quiet, gentle shore of small shingle and sand. Just above the beach are the ruins of a rectangular stone building. This is, or rather was, a haaf station, a seasonal place of refuge and residence from which crews would take fishing boats away offshore to fish the deeper waters – da haaf. Around the building are low, irregular mounds. Where erosion of the beach has cut into these, they can be seen to consist in the main of limpet shells and fish bones, the remnants of bait and processed catch from when the building was in use. Fethaland is a deeply evocative place, the contrasting shores emphasising the power of the prevailing weather in a remote, northerly part of Britain. The islands of Yell and Unst extend further north than Fethaland, but they are more populated and accessible than this bleak, distant spot.

At the other end of Britain, the spit of Dungeness projects into the Channel. This is a temporary coastline *par excellence*, a gravel headland that has probably been forming for several millennia but given a particular boost by destabilisation of the adjacent coastline during major storms in the 13th century. Today it is a stark triangle of shingle, populated by a small number of people, many of whom have chosen it precisely for its other-worldly isolation. An important nature reserve gives some shelter to migrating birds and rare bumble bees, and the tip of the headland boasts a nuclear power station. It is, in many ways, a thoroughly odd place. The beach shelves steeply into deep water and is popular with anglers, and with those who simply want to watch the ships that pass by sometimes surprisingly close inshore. All of that gives Dungeness a particular atmosphere, but it is the sound of the place that sticks in the memory. Even on a calm day, there will be waves beating against the steep shingle banks, the water pushing deep into spaces between the stones before draining back downslope, often moving flint pebbles as it does so. This produces a rushing, hissing sound of water and air pushing through narrow spaces, overlain by the sharp clatter of flint rattling against flint. When the sea is rough and waves a couple of metres high are breaking onshore, the sound is an almost deafening, surging cacophony. There are so many more special stretches of coastline to think about. Places with seabird colonies on cliffs topped by pink thrift, or huge mudflats in winter filling up with vast flocks of hungry wading birds that swirl through the dull sky like flickering smoke. Islands that are almost all edge, where the sea may be in sight in all directions most of the time and it feels as if one huge spring tide could cover the land entirely. There is always something happening at the coast, whether it be holidaymakers thronging Brighton beach, the tide quietly sluicing through the saltmarshes of the Humber estuary, or the Atlantic swell flinging itself against Cornwall. And the sea makes a fine horizon, not a background but an edge of vision beyond which lies the rest of world.

Evening light, falling tide

Home ground

One of the consequences of the 2020 Covid lockdown has been the need to find Outdoor exercise closer to home. Government advice, or possibly regulation, who knows, was not to travel more than short distances in order to have exercise. It is only too obvious that a lot of people ignored this advice, requirement, regulation or law. None the less, for many people this was a time for getting to know their local 'patch', the countryside and footpaths readily accessible from home. This is no bad thing. I am only too well aware of the urge to travel to some well-known beauty spot, passing en route local footpaths that I have never explored. Getting to know one's local patch can be both enjoyable and surprising, and part of an important process of becoming 'grounded' in a place.

'Local patch', looking East towards Otley Chevin

I am very fortunate to have within a few miles of home some particularly fine, diverse patches of Outdoor Yorkshire. It seems only courteous to share a few places with you, to reflect on what makes them special. I don't live in the heart of the countryside, remote from everywhere, up a dirt track and hidden among gnarly old trees. Our home is in what might be called a village, albeit a much expanded one, on the edge of the travel-to-work area north of Leeds and Bradford. We have a railway line, we have buses, we even have a by-pass. It is positively civilised.

To get a feel for the history of the place, join me on the main street, a narrow road that used to be the A65, the major route between Leeds and Kendal. Amble down Iron Row, past a terrace of bijou stone cottages that now fetch silly prices but were built to accommodate home-working weavers. Though small, the cottages have stone internal staircases and stone floors to the upper storey, so that the looms could have a firm footing and good light above street level. We stroll on, passing under the by-pass, then bear left at what was the gatehouse to a large weaving mill complex. The mill closed in the 1960s. When we first moved here, some of the older local women had been mill-workers and retained a personal knowledge of that very distinctive local culture.

We walk on, past an unexpected terrace of Edwardian houses, down a wooded slope, to reach a wide path flanked by trees. To the left is an open field, once the park-like grounds of a mill-owner's house.

Greenholme Mill, a victim of stop-start refurbishment

To the right is a static canal, the Goit, formerly the water-flow that powered the big mill that we can just see through the trees. This path is popular with walkers and joggers. The trees give a fine dappled shade in summer. When the adjacent field is mown, red kites come and quarter it, waiting for the mowers to disturb mice and voles. Traffic noise may be just audible from the by-pass but it takes only a little wind in the trees to hide it.

After a while, the path bends a bit to the left and the Goit has a spur that runs off into the River Wharfe. Originally there was a mill beside this spur: today the water powers an electricity turbine. Cast-iron gateposts on our left show a former entrance to the mill-owner's house, now long gone. There is a small cluster of houses here at the turn of the track, among them a converted barn and small modern cottages built within the former walled garden. Opposite, a steep lane crosses the Goit and goes down to the side of the River Wharfe. To maintain water levels in the Goit, a great weir was built across the Wharfe at this point, utilising a natural step in the sandstone. The weir is a fine feature, gently pouring in the summer, when an astute heron stands at its foot waiting for lunch to be swept past it. There are rocks below the weir, vantage points for grey wagtails and dippers, which nest here some years.

A public footpath crosses the river just below the weir, via a line of stepping stones by which the sure of foot may cross not only the river but the county boundary into North Yorkshire. Visas are not normally required but West Yorkshire residents should take care to leave by sunset. There are plans to put a footbridge across at this point, to encourage more people to cross the river. The first plans for such a bridge were laid in 1918. This is a lovely spot in summer. Sand martins often nest in the bank and whizz around in the evening light, hoovering up insects. A small beach has formed, mostly of pebbles originally brought into the valley by ice then washed down by the river. The pebbles are a cross-section of the upstream geology: smooth, grey limestone, fine sandstones flecked with mica, coarse grits with the texture of flapjack. In the winter, however, the Wharfe is bloated with rain and melted snow from the higher hills and the weir thunders, the stepping stones are overwhelmed. A yellow sign warns against entering fast-flowing water, just in case you fail to notice the seething currents and broken branches whisking away downstream.

Stepping stones across the Wharfe

Head inland from the river and the way rises gently to a higher terrace on which the village is located, safe from the overbank floods for which the Wharfe is notorious. Most winters see us cut off for a day or so as the river stretches itself across the main road on either side of the village. At those times, it is easy to understand the location of the original village centre. Cross the main road and head towards the station. The land rises steadily, houses eventually giving way to pasture fields with sheep and occasional cattle, some fields fenced, others hedged, with mature trees along some of the older boundaries. This is gentle country, easy on the eye.

Gentle country ... easy on the eye

Most of it is lightly grazed and a few curlews generally manage to find a corner to nest, with lapwings flocking here in the winter. Ahead, the fields rise more steeply, to a contouring road along which houses are loosely strung. Above the road, the grassy fields mostly give way to open moorland. A few stone-walled fields high up on the hillside appear to be long-abandoned, their walls tumbling and the land given over to sedge and bracken. These date from the Napoleonic Wars, when anxiety over food security led some land-owners to try 'improving' the land at ever-greater elevations. It was unsustainable and these topmost fields went out of use, left to enwilden themselves. One such field becomes a thing of beauty in May. The field slopes to face northwards and a few scrubby hawthorns and a wall throw more shade onto its uphill end. It is here, where the spring sunshine is diffused a little, that a dense patch of bluebells comes into flower, a contrasting splash on the predominant greens and browns.

Burned, bleak grouse moor

The open moor above should be wild nature at its most natural, but it is not. This is, in a way, a more artificial, man-made landscape than the pasture fields below. Heather, known locally as ling, and bilberry predominate with pale pink tufts of fine-leaved heath along path sides. The vegetation is maintained by grazing sheep in the summer and by burning as grouse-moor management. Its advocates will claim that this management is what maintains the heather plant community so they are helping to conserve something ancient and special. This is, of course, self-serving codswallop of the first order. The pollen record held in bogs across the North shows that heather spread across these hills in the last few centuries BC, a period for which there is no evidence of active grouse-moor management, not even in *Asterix* books. The wide-open, some might say bleak, moorland landscape is an artifice.

There is industrial archaeology here, too, in the form of small reservoirs. Today, they feed water into the grid for this part of Yorkshire, though formerly they maintained the water-level in streams that powered small mills further down the hill. At the very lip of the valley, a long, flat-topped bank looks suspiciously man-made. In fact it isn't. This is a lateral moraine marking the highest point to which ice filled the Wharfe valley around 20,000 years ago. Here and there along the moraine are hollowed-out patches where people have dug out some of the rocks and pebbles that the ice brought from further up the valley – the same pick-and-mix that makes the beach by the weir. Among these scrapes, you may find some grey limestone that is charred, burned. When the highest farmhouses were being built on the sides of the moor, lime was needed for mortar and the most readily available source was to quarry limestone cobbles from the moraine and burn them in temporary kilns. Hence the charred limestone pebbles, which are not, as I was once authoritatively assured they were, meteorites.

Pick a good viewpoint and have a look around. That outcrop of sandstone blocks – the Grubstones – is a good place to sit. To the North, the moor falls away steeply, with bracken and heather giving way to grass then to trees and rooftops. Beyond the river, pasture fields like green tiles with a grouting of trees rise gently to the far skyline, finally giving way to heather. Push on a bit across that hilltop and you are on the evocatively named Blubberhouses Moor. Much fun can be had at the expense of naïve visitors by making up plausible etymologies for this placename that somehow link it to the whaling industry. In fact, 'blubber' derives from 'blaebaer', a local pronunciation of 'bilberry'. But keep that to yourself. North of the river, estates predominate and at least three big houses with their shelter belts and home farms can be picked out. Over to the Northeast, a redundant radio mast marks Norwood Brow. Between here and there, the land folds suddenly downwards into the Washburn valley, which is completely invisible from this angle. A substantial valley with a chain of reservoirs (hence "Valley of the Dammed"), it simply disappears as dead ground over which the eye skims to the higher ground beyond.

Just down the Wharfe valley is the town of Otley, its old centre hardly visible under trees and in shadow, its extension across the river much more obvious. The buildings of Wharfedale Hospital are especially intrusive but it is too precious to be resented, a local resource that reduces the need to travel into either of the big cities. Around to the East, the wooded ridge of Otley Chevin leads the eye to the low-lying Vale of York beyond, with the Yorkshire Wolds distant and grey in the background. Continue round, and the moor slopes away towards Leeds and Bradford, the taller buildings of which can be picked out should the fancy take you. Beyond Bradford, that single spike is the Emley Moor television mast, at 330m tall the UK's premier concrete erection. Keep turning and a flock of wind turbines marks the hill above Ogden Reservoir and the Calder Valley, then Lancashire's Pendle broods sullenly, still sulking over the witches. We come around to the North again, to the white radar balls of Menwith Hill, just West of elegant Harrogate. It is really quite a view, taking in two cities, several power stations distant on the lower Aire and Ouse, and three National Parks: the Yorkshire Dales, North York Moors and the Peak District. I have baked on these rocks on a hot day, jogged up here in thick snow, been here with friends, watched our sons learn to climb. The view has never become familiar and jaded, nor has the sense of being above the world, swept by the wind, hearing meadow pipits, curlews and the occasional golden plover. Despite the smell of burned heather once in a while, it's a good place. In fact, having got up here, why not continue Westwards across the moor, past the stone circle at the 12 Apostles and drop down into Ilkley? Or miss Ilkley and just keep going. It's only, what, 12 miles to Skipton.

That's a brief introduction to my local patch, though there is plenty more that could be mentioned. We populate our local Outdoors with specific places that become significant to us for reasons that would be difficult to explain to someone else, places where something particular happened or that we saw one day in just the right light. There is a spot on the moor where I one day saw the most green hairstreak butterflies that I have ever seen in one place, a flittering kaleidoscope of brilliant metallic green flecks catching the sun. It is just another patch of damp heather moorland, but I know exactly where it is and remember those butterflies whenever I am near that spot. And that is the essence of being Outdoors, experiencing those moments, writing them onto our mental map and being able to recall them. Wordsworth famously wrote about "Emotion recollected in tranquillity" but maybe he had it the wrong way about. What the Outdoors can give us, especially in a local patch that we know very well and in detail, is a recollection of tranquillity when our emotions are most in need of it.

*On Rombald's Moor. A reminder that moorland paths
have been, and some still are, important routeways
between settlements*

Rural nostalgia

One aspect of Outdoors that is seldom the subject of detailed discussion is the association that the British tend to make between the countryside and the past. The connection is so ingrained as to be more or less subconscious, something rarely acknowledged and readily denied. Until, that is, we are strolling through a quiet village in Wessex, admiring the surviving examples of thatched roofs and the carefully-maintained duck-pond, and we find ourselves brought up short, perhaps even tutting audibly, at a proliferation of satellite dishes and a conspicuous ATM. They are an intrusion of a modern world that would be taken for granted in any city into a rural idyll that we would prefer to be fixed in time at least a generation ago. We are nostalgic for an Outdoors that is not of the here and now.

Thatched Devon. The modern context was deliberately not cropped out of the picture

The Welsh language has a useful word 'hiraeth' that refers to a wistfully-recalled past when everything seems somehow to have been better than it is now: a kinder, fairer society, more flowers and birdsong, warmer summers and so on. *Hiraeth* is the nostalgic recollection of a past that probably never existed. Put in those terms it seems harmless enough, if a little wet and pathetic. Dig a little deeper, though, and our rural nostalgia becomes problematic.

When was this golden past? That very much depends on the age of the person whom you ask, because more often than not it turns out to be roughly when they were a young child. You could play out all day and nobody locked their doors, everybody knew their neighbours all down the street. And, of course, as children we were unaware of the social undercurrents, protected from learning about the darker side of those days. Unless our childhoods were truly dreadful, the stuff of best-selling misery lit, it is hardly surprising that our nostalgic baseline is set to a time that we can only vaguely and episodically recall and in which the harsher realities of life passed us by. Do I really want rural Britain to resemble the world of my childhood, in which polio was still a real threat to children, country village schools delivered only the most basic of education, and titled landowners exercised a feudal degree of control over the lives of those who lived on their estates? Not really, no.

Moving from the individual to the collective, there are other, greater dangers in seeing the countryside as a refuge for the Old Ways. One of the things shared by the populist dictators of the 20th century – Hitler, Stalin, Mao, Franco – was their manipulation of rural

118

nostalgia into a political philosophy that painted the cities, with their debauched modern ways and foreign influences, as having a degrading effect on the national soul, while the countryside kept to purer, traditional beliefs and practices. From there, it is just a small step to advocating belief in the true, national patriots who work the land and have always done so, in contradistinction to the shifting cosmopolitans of the cities, whose allegiances are suspect. Nostalgically privileging the imagined culture of a rural tradition rooted in the land is the thin end of a very nasty wedge that has purges and mass graves at its other end.

It may seem to be, and probably is, a long way from Blood and Soil fascism to the British imagery of farmers working the land like their fathers before them to produce food that feeds the nation, and acting as custodians of the countryside to keep it chocolate-box beautiful and, above all, tidy. To question that image almost seems to be wilfully blasphemous, like swearing in church or criticising Judi Dench. However, it shares with Mao and the Third Reich a spurious privileging of country ways as being best, and embedded rural knowledge as being wisdom. One of the consequences is that rural Britain is infantilised, simplified and fossilised by the National Trust and the BBC's *Countryfile* programme, uncritically depicted and always more willing to look back one or two generations than to set out new objectives for the generation ahead. An amiable "Now, your family has farmed this land for over 200 years..." is never followed up with "...so why has such a big soil erosion problem been allowed to develop?" Although I love

Top: Askwith Show 2013
Below: Otley Show 2010.
Smithing competition and
ferret racing.

village shows of the sort in which cattle are shown off, sheep judged and ferrets raced, there is always a nagging little voice that points out how traditional rural crafts are being sanctified. See here, this forging of horseshoes and wickering of baskets, that's proper craftsmanship, not your 3D printing, whatever that is. And, once again, the setting is more or less the idealised childhood decades of the middle-aged people who mostly attend such events.

It is all about baselines and when to set them. At the time of the Brexit farrago, there was much loose talk of reducing Britain's reliance on food imports and EU subsidies and freeing up our farmers to once again feed the nation. A few historians did point out that Britain has needed to import food since at least the late 1700s, when the population was much smaller and the standard of living of most people much lower than it is today. Digging for Victory probably helped a little during World War 2, but it was mostly propaganda. None the less, historical facts notwithstanding, the 'feed the nation' catchphrase gained traction. Can our knowledge of the past help us at all in our management of the countryside? What if we throw the baseline back to the days before industrialised farming? There would be more flowers in the meadows, more wildlife in the hedgerows (which would have to be replanted, come to think of it, having largely been destroyed), much less use of polluting diesel. To take just one consequence of that line of thinking, any such changes to farming would require a lot more people to work the land, and therefore more places for people to live in rural areas. Look at village census data for the era before the large-scale development of commuter belts. Substantial parts of Outdoor Britain would have to become busier, more populated. Beware of unintended consequences!

Historic tractor parade, Warwickshire 2012, with a Little Grey Fergie leading the pack.

I am deeply sceptical about rural nostalgia, as the perceptive reader may have noticed, and that leads me to have reservations about one major current trend in the shaping of the great Outdoors – rewilding. On the face of it, this ought to be a good thing, a planning presumption in favour of repairing centuries of damage, reforesting some of the land, decanalising rivers to allow them to inhabit their flood plains, re-establishing stable populations of formerly native animals. Surely it's all good, so why the grumbly cynicism? It is the first two letters that bother me: RE-wilding. As with return, repeat, renaissance, there is an implication of putting back, or going back to, some previous state of wildness. What previous state and when? As an archaeologist, I am well aware that people have been shaping the landscape and ecology of Britain for thousands of years, so how wild does your 'wild' need to be? The first few millennia of the Holocene, say from 11,000 to 8,000 years ago, were probably splendidly wild, though the human population was numbered in thousands rather than millions. How can we put back to wildness a Britain that contains more people than ever before, in which the land is densely reticulated by roads and railways, and in which soils are older and more exhausted than ever before? The aim of wilding Britain is wholly laudable and achievable: re-wilding carries hints of looking back, with all the attendant problems of baselines and self-deluding nostalgia.

There is a difference, I think between nostalgia and conservation, whether in its cultural or its natural history sense. Conservation has to be based in the here and now, facing up to the likely needs and challenges of the next few decades. A conserved countryside would maintain those elements of it that we value and can see have a purpose in the coming years, but alongside such modernising changes as are necessary to ensure that rural areas can continue to function and develop, to have a future for their resident as well as their visiting populations. So maintain those thatched roofs, not just for their appearance but because a thatched roof provides a range of very particular habitats for invertebrate animals, birds and bats, and welcome the satellite dishes and phone masts that keep people in touch and the ATM machines that sustain the cash economy in places that are unlikely to have a bank branch.

Pragmatic compromise. Abandoned railway near Keswick, Cumbria repurposed as a cycle track and allowed to self-wilden

Natural history conservation needs to adopt a similar degree of pragmatism. By all means use captive breeding and release methods or whatever it takes to rebuild populations of species that have been hard-hit. The loss of water voles in Britain over the last 30 or so years is particularly sad: if captive breeding can halt the decline and even put some of them back where they were previously, that is all to the good. However, remedial works on single species do not constitute wilding. Taking Britain as a whole, the biggest issue with our wildlife is the loss of large apex predators, leading to periodic over-abundance and necessary culling of some herbivores and some local over-abundance of medium-sized predators such as badgers through mesopredator release in the absence of larger species. How would we feel about being Outdoors in

Britain if populations of wolves, lynx and bears were re-established, not simply in order to set-dress the countryside but as keystone species in new, stable ecosystems? We are not accustomed to sharing the landscape with something that could potentially kill us (apart from Friesian cows!), and public reaction to the return of these three species has been tinged with more than a little anxiety. Much the most dangerous would be bears, which are also the least likely to be fitted back into a crowded Britain. Wolves have a scary reputation, thanks to folk stories and horror movies, but are not much of a threat unless seriously short of food and significantly encroached upon. By and large, wolves have the sense to avoid people. Lynx would be much the easiest to accommodate, and at the time of writing their re-introduction to Britain seems likely to be at least trialled in the near future. Good.

For those of us who value the Outdoors and want to spend time there, the immediate future presents two challenges. The first is to cut through the thick web of nostalgia. The past certainly was a different country, and it has gone. Speaking as an archaeologist once again, I am very aware that we operate in the contemporary landscape: archaeologists do not study the past because it has gone beyond observation or recall. We study those traces of the past that persist in the present landscape. That approach needs to replace the maudlin nostalgia that somehow thinks that 'the past' can be retained or rebuilt in some kind of totality. We live in the present landscape. If we want thatched roofs and water voles, then let us conserve them. If we want near-feudal management and minimal conservation oversight of large shooting estates, then make that a positive decision and not some kind of default to which we resort because "That's how it has always been hereabouts". Rural nostalgia suits those who have 'always' had the casting vote over the management and use of Outdoor Britain, because that management has largely been to their benefit. It suits those of a conservative (small c, please note) political hue as well, as it harks back to a world in which children were rosy-cheeked, not brown-skinned, in which issues around the vexed topic of immigration were something that affected the towns. One of the most welcome changes that I have seen in this part of Yorkshire over the last 20 years is the increasing number of people apparently of British-Asian origin who are not merely visiting the Outdoors but thoroughly engaging with it, becoming part of that community of walkers, runners, painters, botanists and birders. The second challenge is to accept that the form and function of Outdoors in 20 years' time is in our hands now and that it requires decisions to be formulated and implemented, based on the widest possible discussion of what people of all ages and backgrounds want when they spend time Outdoors, and how those wants may best be met and balanced. Retreating into soggy nostalgia will simply be to pass the buck and to miss the opportunity.

Whose Outdoors is it anyway?

Maybe it's my age, maybe it's the age we live in, but I have of late become increasingly grumpy and critical of the ways in which just being Outdoors in the Britain has become a packaged commodity for which we have to pay in a host of different ways. On the other hand, being a reasonable chap, I can see why this situation has arisen and don't necessarily resent all of the pockets into which that money goes. Tricky, isn't it? Let's try to tease this apart.

*Chatsworth House, seat of the Dukes of Devonshire.
The Estate covers some 14,000 hectares across
Cheshire and Staffordshire, and the family owns
another 12,000 hectares in Yorkshire.
Photo: Sonia O'Connor*

First of all, more or less the whole of Britain is owned by somebody: private landowners, hedge funds, the Queen, the Church, insurance companies. Areas of true common land, owned by some civic authority or charity on behalf of every one, are rare and precious. The National Trust hold a lot of land in trust for the nation, though much of that is then leased out. What this creates is an immediate source of potential conflict between those who own or lease the land and those who want access to it for rest and recreation. In effect, this has its origins in the Parliamentary Enclosures of the late 18th and 19th centuries, in which, depending on your point of view, responsible landowners took over areas of badly-maintained common land to ensure that it was farmed efficiently or rich people with influence stole common land from the poor and disenfranchised. That process, in turn, could be seen as a repeat of the carving-up of England that followed the Norman take-over after 1066. Countryside access conflicts have deep roots.

Second, farm incomes in Britain have, by and large, been depressed and fluctuating since the 1960s. Land is the farmer's stock in trade, so it is not unreasonable that land owners and their tenants should utilise that land in whatever ways allow them to make a living. This adds another layer of conflict to the whole debate, namely that between the needs of small farmers, especially upland livestock farmers, and the commercial farming concerns who run much of the arable farming of the lowlands. What is good for the latter is not necessarily to the benefit of the former, but it is the latter group that have the ear of Government.

Understandably mixed messages: signs in a farm gateway and outside a pub, Malham, Yorkshire

The most obvious point at which we meet the commoditisation comes if we drive into the countryside in order to get into wide open spaces for a day out. Where do we park? Not in field gateways, obviously, nor on narrow lanes. I have nothing but sympathy for farmers and other country residents who get steamed up over the blithering idiocy of a minority of drivers, whose inability to think about the obstruction and hazard that their ill-parked vehicles might cause is quite jaw-dropping. So the provision of car-parking areas in popular places serves everybody's purposes, and it is not unreasonable to ask for some contribution towards the costs of upkeep. Fine, that's a fair deal. But the level of charging for a day's parking in some places is positively eye-watering, way beyond what might be thought reasonable. So people try to avoid paying for parking and block gateways and narrow lanes. A further step in the escalation comes when landowners try to make it impossible not to pay their high parking charges by blocking and obstructing potential roadside parking places, even where parking would be completely unproblematic. That's the point at which my inner Leveller rises up and reaches for the pitchfork.

But country folk have to make a living! Why shouldn't visitors to the countryside make a contribution to the incomes of the people who look after the land, year round, through thick and thin? That's an easy argument to make. Speaking personally I would rather pay a couple of quid directly to a farmer in order to park on her land than paying several times as much to the National Trust, English Heritage or Bolton Abbey Estate for the use of a car-park. At least I could see where the money was going. The problem is that British taxpayers already make a substantial contribution to the incomes of country folk. Those small upland farms that dot our National Parks would largely be bankrupt without taxpayer support, whether in the form of direct support payments or charges not taken such as tax-free diesel fuel. In the run-up to the Countryside Rights of Way Act, I was at a discussion meeting held in one of our National Parks. One local farmer voiced the opinion of many when he asked "What gives folk the right to come wandering all over my land?". A voice from the back (not mine) shouted the answer "Two billion quids' worth of subsidies every year, that's what". To the credit of some Yorkshire farmers, several of them spoke up in agreement with the heckler. The outbreak of foot and mouth disease that ripped through the British countryside in 2001 brought a number of things to the public attention for the first time. The level of subsidies was one. Another was the way in which farming, the industry in which the damaging incident had originated, was the only rural industry that was fully compensated for its losses. What happened to the 'polluter pays' principle? Time has passed, but it is possible to see something of a shift in attitudes deriving from the CRoW Act and the fallout from foot and mouth. People started to ask rather pointed questions about why countryside access was being sold back to the very people who were effectively paying for it in the first place.

Lower Winskill, Yorkshire. How are hill farms such as this to make a living and support conservation?
Photo: Sonia O'Connor

If the public at large are paying for the countryside, what are they getting for it? Food is the answer that is most often given, though that barely stands up to close scrutiny in a world in which food resources are shipped around at the behest of market forces, just another commodity from which to skim a profit as it moves from hand to hand. Farmers' markets are largely separate from that system and actually do represent a fairly direct supply chain from farm to consumer, though they also represent a tiny proportion of the total market, satisfying but commercially irrelevant. In any case, if the priority were to produce food, the countryside would be farmed much more intensively. At this point, the discussion shifts its position to the 'custodians of the countryside' model. Farming a little less than efficiently maintains the beautiful landscapes that people want to see when they come Outdoors for rest and recreation.

The problem with this line of argument, I think, is that the public are so often told that this is the countryside they want, rather than being asked what they want and engaged in a serious discussion about the use of the countryside. There is a counter-argument to that, too, that says that townsfolk (i.e. anyone not a farmer) don't understand the countryside and should leave its management to farmers. There may be an element of truth in that, but when it is 'townsfolk' who are both the customers and the subsidisers of the countryside, it strikes me a highly vulnerable case to make. Just keep paying the piper and leave the choice of tunes to us.

This is the nub of the problem. The public are sold a commodity in the making of which they have little say and in which they have already made a substantial investment. It is a recipe for misunderstanding and discontent on all sides. To be fair, some farmers and landowners are very well aware of this ambiguity and are responsive to public opinions and needs. The best of them do an outstanding job, and I have the greatest respect for them. What is lacking is a general shift of perspective, such that those responsive farmers become the majority, the default position, not a scatter of outstanding individuals. And on the other side, it would certainly help if more people spent more time Outdoors with their eyes and ears open to what happens around them. Even that becomes difficult when access means driving to a large car-park and joining a clutter of others on a well-maintained footpath, eventually stopping for tea at a café, the clientele of which is entirely visitors. It is as if two worlds move through and past each other without making contact. Yes, many townsfolk do not understand the countryside, but it is equally true that many farmers and other rural workers do not understand the larger world. Generalisations both, with exceptions on both sides, but there is some truth in it.

The development of 'honeypot' locations is part of the problem. Every National Park or beauty spot has its foci, where parking and tea-shops proliferate and at which visitors congregate. In this part of Yorkshire, the village of Grassington is one such place, equipped with a huge car park on its edge and its steep, narrow streets lined with tea-shops, gift-shops and trinket-mongers. Wander through Grassington on a summer's day and it would be easy to mistake it for a theme park, which would not necessarily be an error. How could you find out what it is like to live in such a place? Head off down a side-street and knock on the door of a small cottage? It's worth a try, but the cottage would almost certainly be a holiday let, currently occupied by a nice family from Basingstoke. The same could be said of so many other locations around Britain, places that are entirely tailored to serving the needs of, and earning money from, visitors. What they deliver to the visitor is a packaged Outdoors, made convenient and shaped to a particular perception of what it is the visitor wants. What they all too often do not deliver is any sense of being in a real place where people live and with which those people have an engagement that goes beyond selling you an ice cream or a parking permit.

What's to be done? The answer to that would have to involve national politics and, at the time of writing, the governance of Britain is lying dead in a ditch having been assaulted and robbed. Positive change will not come from the top down. A few hero farmers take on projects to enhance the biodiversity of their land, aware that this will probably bring more people to the tea-table and jam sales, but also taking on the work because of a sense that it is the right thing to do. More power to them. Those of us who spend time Outdoors could do more, too. Avoid the honeypots, try to find genuinely local shops rather than the visitor-facing ones. Chat to locals should you happen across them. I learned something important about Yorkshire farmers from a chance conversation with one around a decade ago. He was leaning on a gate gazing at his cattle as I stepped over the adjacent stile. I commented that cattle were an unusual sight in that region. "Aye. That's the last dairy herd in Upper Wharfedale." "How do you make dairying pay these days" I asked, naively. "I don't" he said, "But I like cows". It was a good reminder that commercial logic is not the only factor in deciding how land is managed and farmed. We have to remember that when pressing for roadside verges to remain unmown or for hill pastures to be taken out of grazing so that scrub habitats can establish. The people who will be asked (expected, told, paid) to implement any such changes of management will have an emotional attachment to the land as it is, or as it was, a sense of 'this is how it should look'. That attachment has to be turned into engagement with the proposed changes, and that will be much easier in some cases than in others.

So whose Outdoors is it? Everyone's, or so it should be, as every taxpayer in Britain pays in to the upkeep of the countryside and those who live in it. That doesn't mean we can simply undo the Enclosures and throw huge areas back into common ownership, but it does require that the two communities of residents and visitors make every effort to engage with and to understand each other. It also requires that planning authorities accept that outdoor rest and recreation are national essentials, an investment in people's physical and mental health every bit as important as another field of barley or grazing for another few hundred sheep. And that Outdoors needs to be shared, not only between its human residents and visitors, but with its livestock and wildlife as well. We teach our children to share yet seem to forget about it as adults when it comes to making room for other species or other people's needs and interests. Reshaping a fragmented commodity as a national asset is unlikely to be seen as a priority by national politicians so will have to be done from the bottom upwards, a grass-roots movement in every possible sense.

Climber enjoying the Outdoors at Almscliff Crag, Yorkshire. Photo courtesy of James O'Connor